Harmony

Analyzing the Music of Elton John, 1968-1977

Scott Robinson

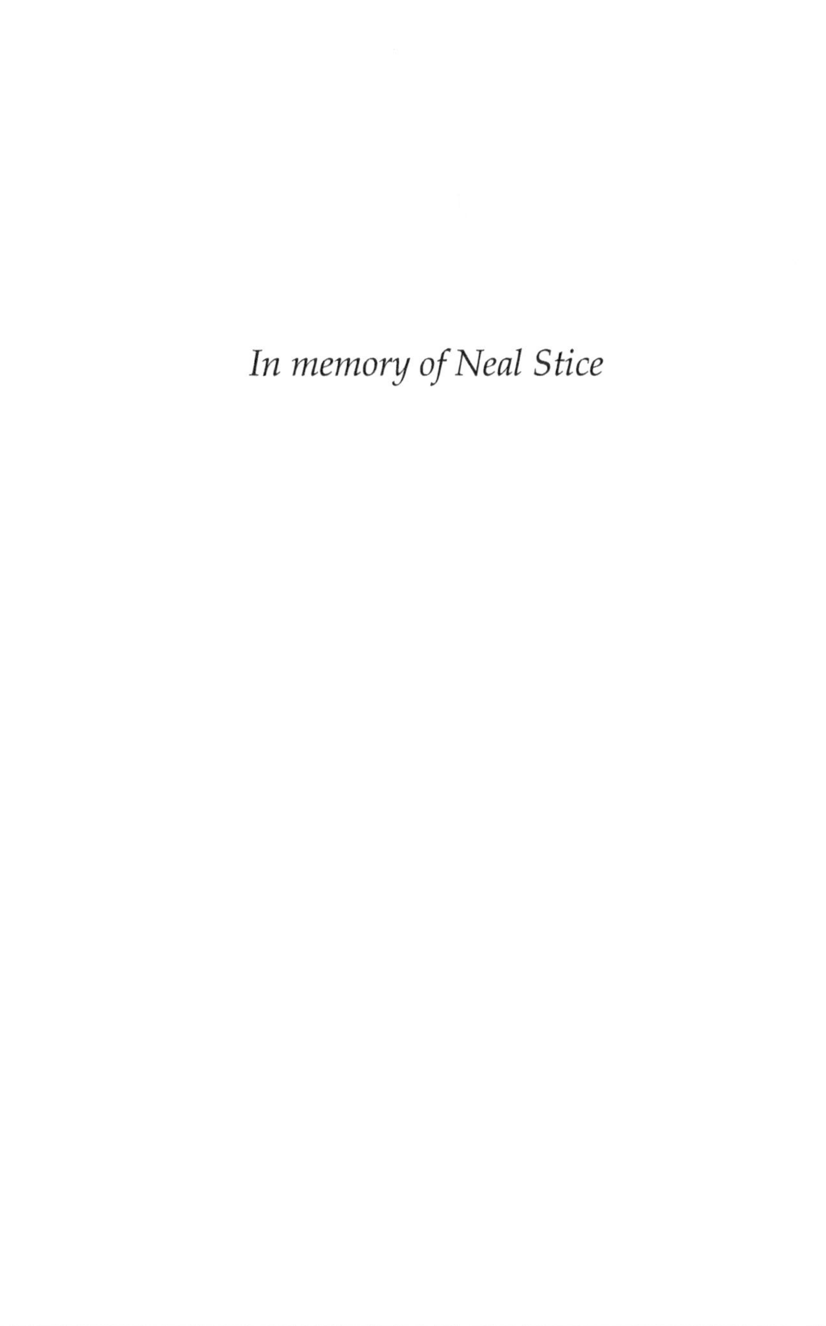

In memory of Neal Stice

Also by Scott Robinson ...

AI in Sci-Fi: Fictional Artificial Minds
        and the Real World Awaiting Them
The Children of Babel: Essays on the Inherent Nature of
        Artificial Intelligence and Consciousness
A Conversation with Hofstadter's Brain
HAL 9000: An Unauthorized Biography
Red Brains, Blue Brains:
        Neuroscience and Donald Trump
Red Brains, Blue Brains: Authoritarian We Will Go!
A Chill in the Air: Profiles in American Authoritarianism
The Smell of the Lord:
        Growing Up Fundamentalist in the American Midwest
Lucy's Courtship: An Integrated Perspective
        on the Feminine Role in Human Sexual Evolution
Really Great Things That I Didn't Say
The 21st Century Grown-Ass Man:
        A No-Nonsense Guide for the Middle-Aged Emotional Survivalist
The Heart of the Scots:
        Love, Sex and Romance in Scottish History
A Dark and Stormy Night in Scotland!
        Folk Tales, Legends, and Disturbing Bedtime Stories
        for the True Believer
Uncle Scott's Treasury of Useless Knowledge
Uncle Scott's Treasury of Random Information
Chasing the Enterprise:
        Achieving *Star Trek*'s Vision of the Human Future
Rock Candy: The Beatles
Rock Candy: Elton John
The Quotable Beatles
To the Toppermost of the Poppermost:
        The #1 Hits of the Beatles, Before and After
The Progressive Beatles
YesTales: An Unauthorized Biography
        of Rock's Most Cosmic Band
This Is What I'm Saying:
        Burdens of a Midwestern Suburban Polymath
My Work Here is Done!
        More Very Random Essays on Weighty Matters
I Think I'm Right in Saying That?
        The Intellectual Chaos Continues!
Why Is He Telling Us These Things?
        The Best of Uncle Scott, 2012-2020

Table of Contents

Introduction

Rock music, for me, began on a school bus when I was 10 years old.

Elton

Reginald Dwight was born on March 25, 1947, into a musical family.

His father Stanley was a squadron leader in the Royal Air Force – but he also played trumpet with Bob Miller and the Millermen. His mother Sheila worked for a dairy company – but she was Reg's first fan, along with her mother Ivy and sister Win. And at 55 Pinner Hill Road, where they lived with Sheila's parents, the radio was the go-to family entertainment. Reg – who would, of course, one day become Elton - would sit with them and listen to Sinatra, Nat King Cole, George Shearing, Rosemary Clooney; and his parents had a formidable record collection, including Les Paul and Guy Mitchell and Frankie Lane and Tennessee Ernie Ford and Jo Stafford and Johnny Ray and Mary Ford.

The adult Elton would one day credit that musical environment – and his mother's support, in particular – for making him the musician he became. "My mother introduced me to rock 'n' roll," he said in 1971. "One day she came home with 'ABC Boogie' by Bill Haley and 'Heartbeat Hotel' by Elvis Presley. She has always been well up on what's going on."

The family seemed to predestine Reg for a musical life. He was scarcely more than a toddler when he began picking out tunes on the family piano. But there was much more going on in his early years besides music – and not much of it good.

History describes Stanley as distant and uninvolved with Reg, an only child. Elton himself claimed on a number of occasions that he didn't even bother returning from assignment to see his son until he was two years old. "My dad never saw me for two years," he said in a 1976 Playboy interview. "I was two years old when he came home from the Air Force. He'd never seen me. And it got off to a really bad start, because Mother said, 'Do you want to go upstairs and see him?' Father said, 'No, I'll wait till morning.'"[1]

---

[1] It turns out this isn't true. Biographer Philip Norman determined that Stanley Dwight was in fact on home posting with an RAF maintenance unit nearby. He was home when Reg was born, registered his son's birth the next day, and came home each evening the first 18 months of Reg's life.

Biographer Philip Norman assesses Stanley's attitude toward his son not as aloofness but as a counterbalance to the overwhelmingly female atmosphere of the household; and he chronicles Stanley's own bewilderment at Elton's tirades against him in the press in later decades, characterizing him as cold[2], when in fact he had worked hard to connect with his young son when he would return after months away on assignment.

Whatever balance he may have been trying to impart in Elton's life, however, was shattered in any case by the cacophony of the quarrels he and Sheila were constantly engaged in.

"My parents used to argue a lot when I was young," he said in 1997. "I would lock myself in my bedroom. My father would come home and there would be a row. I expected it. And lived in fear of it.

"I don't think I had a dysfunctional background," he said, "but when your parents aren't getting on you tend to go into your own world. Mine was music, and that became my life."

Throughout his childhood, Reg was a loner, never part of a group. "I think being raised by women shaped my personality because I spent a lot of time on my own, in my room, playing records," he said. "It made me a loner. It made me shy with other kids. I created my own world. I was immersed in music and records even at that young age."

Life at 55 Pinner Hill Road, then, propelled Reg Dwight into his future in more ways than one.

The Royal Academy

The movie *Rocketman* endearingly shows Elton sitting down at the piano as a young boy, picking out tunes by ear. Both of his parents had musical ability and had an impressive record collection, so Elton's exposure to music early on was substantial.

---

[2] When Stanley was accidentally electrocuted in 1958, spending months in hospital recovery, neither his wife nor Reg visited even once; when he died in 1991, Elton did not bother to attend his funeral.

At age 7 he began taking piano lessons, and his range was staggering for a pre-teen; he could easily handle the technical intricacies of classical music, but he was just as capable of playing Jerry Lee Lewis – and he already demonstrated a capacity for composition.

At age 11, he was awarded a junior scholarship to the Royal Academy of Music, where he showed his instructor, Helen Piena, that he could play back classical songs he'd never heard before with perfect accuracy.

"I always called him Reginald," she recalled. "He was about eleven when I first met him, and he was charming. When he went away on holiday he always used to bring me a present back. He used to send me postcards with kisses on them. It was a very nice togetherness, really. He was plump, but not overweight. He wore ordinary teenagers' clothes. I mean, teenagers weren't teenagers then, they were just children growing up, and that's what he was – a nice boy. We got on well together. I'm very fond of him."

Piena started Reginald off with Handal, and recalled discovering his replay ability: "I remember playing him one piece four pages long and he played it back to me like a gramophone record," she said. "He had an absolutely extraordinary, wonderful ear. And I never played to him again, ever, because he had to learn to do it himself. He had this wonderful ear but he could not read one note of music. That's the first thing I had to teach him."

He continued at the academy for another five years, attending on Saturdays. His favorite classical composers were Bach and Chopin. But his interest ended there.

"He got on very well until he was about fourteen, which is a crucial age," said Piena. "About that time he began to realize what it was he wanted to do. He told me afterwards that he had formed a jazz band of his own and that's what he was doing. He wasn't doing very much for me."

"I kind of resented going to the Academy," he said. "I was one of those children who could just about get away without practicing and still pass, scrape through the grades."

"I used to look at him on the stool next to me," Piena remembered. "I remember sitting there for three-quarters of an hour trying to persuade him to go to university. And he said, 'No, none of my family has ever been to university. I'm not going to university.' And I couldn't make him change his mind."

He left the Academy without taking his final exams.

"I'm very glad to have had the experience of having a classical background," Elton said later, "because it makes you appreciate all sorts of music. It also helps you as a writer because, as a keyboard player, you tend to write with more chords than a guitar, and I think that has a lot to do with my piano playing and my love of Chopin, Bach, and Mozart and my love of singing in a choir. I think my songs have more of a classical leaning to them than other artists who haven't had that classical background, and I am grateful for that."

"I think his gift is to be able to stand in front of a crowd and talk to them. I think that's a wonderful gift to have," said Piena. However, if you come to the Royal Academy of Music, you expect to learn classical music and be able to perform and play these wonderful things that famous people play, and he didn't do any of this. So, from that point of view, I failed."

After Elton became famous, someone gave his former instructor a tape of his music.

"I didn't play it," she said. "I couldn't face it."

Bluesology

When Reg Dwight was a young teen, he and his neighbor Stu Brown, along with friends Rex Bishop and Mick Inkpen formed a band – Bluesology, stealing the name from the Modern Jazz Quartet and Django Reinhardt.

By the time Reg was 15, Bluesology was playing pubs, including the Establishment Club in London. A couple of years later, Bluesology signed a contract to back American performers, including Patti LaBelle and the Isley Brothers.

Fontana Records signed Bluesology, and Elton (still Reg!) wrote a song called "Come Back Baby" that the band recorded and released. "Mr. Frantic" followed; both songs tanked.

Along comes Long John Baldry, who asks Bluesology to become his backing band. Only Elton and his old friend Stu think that's a good idea, and they re-staff with a new bass player and drummer, a new guitarist, Elton Dean on sax and a trumpet player and an extra vocalist.

Bluesology cut a single, "Since I Found You Baby", for Polydor, and did a session at Abbey Road with Little Richard, recording four songs (and releasing two of them). But as Long John's music swayed toward cabaret, Elton/Reg became tired of the band (he was also now in Bernie's world, which surely pulled him away) - and he, Brown, and Dean all bandoned Bluesology, which disbanded permanently a year later[3].

---

[3] One of the remaining Bluesology players was guitarist Caleb Quaye, who would play on Elton's early albums, and become a full-time band member in the shake-up of 1975.

Bernie

Elton and Bernie Taupin wrote 20 songs together before they'd even met.

Each had seen an ad in the paper from Liberty Records – LIBERTY WANTS TALENT! ARTISTES/COMPOSERS/SINGER-MUSICIANS TO FORM NEW GROUP, referring interested parties to Ray Williams at *New Musical Express*. And each had responded[4].

Ray Williams received both applications, and he was impressed with both Elton (still Reg at that point) and Bernie. But he felt that neither was a complete songwriter. It was his innovation to put the two of them together: he sent a batch of Bernie's lyrics to Elton – and that's how the first 20 songs got written.

Bernie Taupin grew up in the county of Lincolnshire, an undistinguished quarter of England that nonetheless provided him with a happy rural childhood, to which he would constantly be referring back. His was a childhood of innocence and wonder; like Elton, he grew up brotherless, and his great happiness was Sunday matinees, where he received a steady diet of Westerns, and became fascinated with a mythological interpretation of America. Entire Elton albums would one day gravitate to this theme.

And he had tremendous support: "I was blessed with really, really great parents, parents that never challenged me, never asked me why I did what I did," he once said. "They were always there, backing me up."

In the Taupin household, as in the Dwight residence, music reigned. Bernie grew up hearing Johnny Cash, Marty Robbins, Johnny Horton and countless others. His great enthusiasm was for songs that told

---

[4] In Bernie's case, it was one of those things that seems like fate: he had written an application for the position of songwriter to submit to Liberty, put it in an envelope, then tossed it in a trash can. His mother found it and dropped it in a mailbox. Can you imagine what the world would be like if she hadn't?

stories – which, of course, he himself mastered. When Dick James offered him a staff position, he was over the moon.

"To actually be given money for writing songs!" Bernie said. "I couldn't believe they were really serious."

Elton and Bernie, having already written together remotely, met for the first time in Dick James' studio.

"One day I was doing a demo session and I noticed him in the corner," Elton said. "I said, 'Oh, are you the lyric writer?' and he said, 'Yeah,' and we went round the corner for a cup of coffee and that was it, really."

They quickly became best friends. Bernie moved into the city, bunking with Elton at his parents' home. Because of their differing background, Elton became the 'town mouse', while Bernie was the 'country mouse'.

Life as DJM songwriters, before Elton started doing their songs himself, had its interesting turns. Biographer Philip Norman wrote that Paul McCartney would, from time to time, drop by DJM's studio to record with his discovery Mary Hopkin:

"We were there talking to the Barren Knights," Bernie remembered. "Suddenly Paul came in, sat down at the piano and asked us if we'd like to hear this new thing he'd written. It was 'Hey Jude'. God, we thought that was just so cool."

It wasn't long before Elton became engaged to Linda Woodrow, an ill-fated coupling if ever there was one. Elton and Linda rented a basement flat – and Bernie tagged along, That didn't go well at all; Bernie didn't think much of Linda, and it ended in disaster. Elton and Bernie ended up returning to Elton's mother's home.

When their songs turned out to be amazing but not portable to other artists, it became clear that Elton would be performing them – which was a great success. Bernie absorbed this philosophically:

"You have to remember that '69, '70, really really was the beginning of the 'singer-songwriter'," he said. "There was James Taylors, the

Randy Newmans, the Harry Nillsons, the Joni Mitchells, Van Morrison –
I mean, the list is endless. And I think the interesting thing is, outside
of probably Cat Stevens, we were the only English export."

Once it was public knowledge that Elton was gay, there was much
speculation that he and Bernie had been bed partners as well as
songwriting partners.

"I loved Bernie," Elton said. "Not in any physical way. It was just
fantastic to know that someone else knew how I felt." But lovers? "No,
absolutely not. Everybody thinks we were, but if we had been, I don't
think we would have lasted so long. We're more like brothers than
anything else. The press probably thought John Reid and I were an
affair, but there's never been a serious person the whole time."

On *Captain Fantastic*, the biographical story of their relationship,
there's a song called "We All Fall in Love Sometimes", which takes
them back to "Your Song".

Elton: "He loved me. We hit rock bottom together so many times, and
at that point in my life he was the only person I could really call a
friend. We found a spark together, and a way of writing that's still with
us."

And so began years of writing, recording, and touring, during which
Bernie – who could easily have just stayed at home and phoned in his
lyrics – remained constantly at Elton's side.

"I don't think that Bernie ever really liked the fame," Elton said. "He
was always the quiet one and the more thoughtful one. I was always
the one that said, 'Let's go out!' I used to go out with Divine and dance
at clubs. We'd both burn the candle at both ends, but I did it far more
than he did."

But eventually, they needed to put their partnership aside. It happened
after the album *Blue Moves* in 1976.

"In the early days, [Bernie and I] shared a rapport," Elton told the
press. "But it had fallen away."

Rock historian David Buckley notes that Bernie could no longer produce what Elton needed: "Bernie had lost all the buoyancy of his teenage self. Still only twenty-six, he was entering a life-changing period."

Bernie himself saw it differently. "By that point, we seemed to have achieved everything there was to achieve," he said. "Elton had filled every major stadium in the world. We'd written strings of #1s – eventually, things that went into the charts at #1. You couldn't fart without hearing Elton John. At that point, it felt like there was no way we could go any further. There was only one way to go from here."

Bernie went off to get sober and write with other artists, notably Alice Cooper (he also co-wrote the Eighties mega-hit "We Built This City" for Starship).

Five years passed, and Elton's fortunes plummeted. Switching to the Geffen label, it was decided that after the failure of the albums *The Fox* and *Jump Up!*, the thing to do to set the ship right was to get the old band back together: Dee and Nigel, who had been dismissed in 1975, were invited back – and so was Bernie.

"I told Elton, 'We've got to collaborate totally, or it's never going to be any good,'" Bernie said. "To me, our songs have always worked in total, with a feeling of continuity between them. I didn't want to keep on doing odd or obscure tracks on albums of other people's work. We had to try to get back to that complete closeness and understanding we had when we started out."

"It was a healthy time apart," Elton said of their break. "If we hadn't had that break, we might never have survived."

The new album was *21 at 33*, for which Bernie wrote four songs - sharing the lyrics chores on the album with Gary Osborne, who had become Elton's partner after his 1976 departure.

One of those songs, "Two Rooms at the End of the World", was about their partnership. It includes the line, "together the two of them were mining gold."

Two Rooms

The process by which Elton and Bernie created their songs is now legend: Bernie would create a batch of lyrics in solitude, writing them out, and would give the pages to Elton – who, on his own, would create music to go with the words. The two never sat down together, never worked simultaneously. They literally created the music in two rooms.

"Lyrics are always first," Elton told *Circus* magazine just after *Goodbye Yellow Brick Road*'s release. "If I don't have the lyrics I don't write any songs. If Taupin is barren, that's that."

Elton: "I really don't know where his lyrics come from. I was just the guy who wrote the melodies, that was my job. I just love writing to his lyrics. I really don't analyze them much. He's never told me what sort of song to write. He just gave me the lyrics. It's nice when you're creating something that comes together like a jigsaw puzzle very quickly."

Davey: "Elton would have a stack of lyrics and he'd just look through them. He wouldn't do any pre-work in those days; he wouldn't ever sneak 'em at home, he'd wait till he'd get to the studio and then literally sit down after breakfast and write a song. I mean I've seen him write a song in the time it's taken me to make a chicken sandwich."

"The nature of Bernie and Elton's relationship is completely unique, really, in modern rock and roll terms," said rock journalist Robert Sandall. "It had its antecedents in Broadway, probably, but this sort of 'you wash, I'll dry' arrangement that they had, whereby Bernie Taupin would just send Elton John the lyrics - they wouldn't even sit down and say, 'Hey, Elton, here's a lyric – what do you think?'"

"I was just lucky to find somebody who could write lyrics, because I could never have gotten them together. We've been through so many funny things together, so many hard times and disappointments, that we're sort of like brothers, really. All his lyrics are just talking fantasies, so all I'm doing, in fact, is singing Bernie's fantasies. I know that and I enjoy it. I didn't meet him until I'd written the music to about ten of his lyrics."

"I was never interested in writing lyrics, because I never really thought I was any good at it. I knew I could write melodies, and I liked Bernie's lyrics, so I just sort of left it at that. And that's the way it's stayed, really." ~Elton

"To me, there's no such thing as a hit lyric. There are hit melodies - which, if you're lucky, you'll get a great lyric that'll go with it. People don't listen to records for the lyric; if they like the record enough because they like the feel of it or they like the melody, then they'll start to listen to the lyric." ~Gus

"There were a lot of great lyrics around in the early Seventies, records like Don McLean's 'American Pie', 'Vincent' - they were songs that made it on the lyric as much as the tune. And I think the great thing about the songwriting of Elton and Bernie is that it's an equal balance: one is not dominating the other." ~Tim Rice

Bernie: "At that point in time, my musical odyssey hadn't developed enough where I felt confident enough to dictate to him how I felt songs should sound. I gave them to him and kind of ran away."

"He [Bernie] only writes about personal things, which is great. Because I know him inside out and when I get the lyrics I know exactly what he's talking about."

Elton: "Bernie would have a bunch of lyrics, and I would write to about ninety percent of his lyrics back then. There weren't that many of the lyrics discarded."

Elton: "I really don't know what's going on in Bernie's mind. I ask him if a certain song is about a certain person or something like that, but I don't get any sense out of him."

The Forgotten Songs

Pre- "Your Song"

Skyline Pigeon

Lady Samantha

It's Me That You Need

Bad Side of the Moon

Rock and Roll Madonna

Elton John: The Album

Produced by	Gus Dudgeon
Engineered by	Robin Geoffrey Cable
Performed by	Elton John (vocals, piano) Nigel Olsson (drums, vocals) Caleb Quaye (electric guitar) Frank Clark (acoustic guitar, double bass) Colin Green (guitar, Spanish guitar) Clive Hicks (acoustic guitar, rhythm guitar, 12-string guitar) Roland Harker (guitar) Alan Parker (rhythm guitar) Dave Richmond (bass) Alan Weighall (bass) Les Hurdle (bass) Terry Cox (drums) Barry Morgan (drums) Diana Lewis (Moog synthesizer) Brian Dee (organ) Dennis Lopez (percussion) Tex Navarra (percussion) Skaila Kanga (harp) Paul Buckmaster (cello, orchestration) Madeline Bell, Tony Burrows, Roger Cook, Lesley Duncan, Kay Garner, Tony Hazzard, Barbara Moore (backing vocals)
Released	4/10/1970
Chart Position	#4 (US Billboard 200) / #5 (UK Albums)
Sales	Gold (US)
Singles	"Border Song" "Your Song"

An argument can be made, despite 1969's *Empty Sky*, that *Elton John* was his first true album.

It was the first album to have a genuine hit song ("Your Song"). It was the first to showcase his stylistic range. It was the first to unpack Bernie's emotive portraits and intimately personal themes.

"There aren't any forgotten gems on *Empty Sky*," wrote AllMusic's reviewer, "but it does suggest John's potential."

Elton John, on the other hand, not only puts up "Your Song", but two additional Elton gems - "Border Song" and "Take Me to the Pilot", both have which stand up well even today.

Moreover, since *Empty Sky* wasn't released in the US until 1975, *Elton John* was his first appearance in the US – where he took off in the first place.

It's here that the newcomer can truly meet the early Elton.

Tracks

Side One
>**Your Song** (EJ/Taupin) - 4:02
>**I Need You to Turn To** (EJ/Taupin) - 2:35
>**Take Me to the Pilot** (EJ/Taupin) - 3:47
>**No Shoe Strings on Louise** (EJ/Taupin) - 3:31�
>**First Episode at Hienton** (EJ/Taupin) - 4:48�

Side Two
>**Sixty Years On** (EJ/Taupin) - 4:35
>**Border Song** (EJ/Taupin) - 3:22
>**The Greatest Discovery** (EJ/Taupin) - 4:12
>**The Cage** (EJ/Taupin) - 3:28
>**The King Must Die** (EJ/Taupin) - 5:23

The Writing

Bernie's lyrics went everywhere. From the gentle intimacy of "Your Song" to the autobiography in "The Greatest Discovery" (about the birth of Bernie's little brother) to the wistful "First Episode at Heinton", he is at his most emotionally open; at the same time, his dramatic flare is burning bright on "Sixty Years On" and "The King Must Die", which would both be perfectly at home on a theater stage.

Then there's "Border Song", to which Elton actually added lyrics (the "let us live in peace" verse is his). And "Take Me to the Pilot", an early example of Bernie's capacity for writing an image-laden song while completely obscuring its meaning.

The Music

Elton pulled out all the stylistic stop, going mellow on "Your Song", bombastic on "The King Must Die", rock-gospel on "Take Me to the Pilot" - he and Bernie had the courage of their convictions, as well as unshakeable confidence in one another.

Paul Buckmaster, the album's orchestrator: "With each song I heard on the demo, my level of enthusiasm went up and up and up. I was just bopping with excitement to be involved in this project. Elton had decided not to be at all involved in the creative process of how we were going to arrange these songs. He put it entirely into my hands and Gus's hands, so Gus and I had two meetings where we went through all the material we were going to record. We each had a copy of the lyric sheet and went through each song on his desk with a fine-toothed comb."

The Recording

The first choice for producer was George Martin, who had done so much for the Beatles and who had his own studio (AIR). But he insisted on arranging as well as producing, and DJM's Steve Brown wanted those two roles to be individually manned. He turned to Paul Buckmaster, who had done David Bowie's "Space Oddity" for the arranging; Buckmaster, in turn, introduced him to Gus Dudgeon. Dudgeon was excited about working with Elton upon hearing the demos, just as Buckmaster had been.

"To play with a live orchestra was extremely intimidating," Elton said. It was quite a fearsome task, but we did it. Gus Dudgeon produced and the team was born. It was just like Bernie and me; it was fate, basically."

Playing harpsichord on "I Need You to Turn To" was a particular challenge: "While it looks very similar to the pianoforte, there is a delay to how the mechanism works so it is very easy to fuck it all up if you're not thinking ahead. "

The Response

John Mendelsohn, *Rolling Stone*: "The major problem with *Elton John* is that one has to wade through so damn much fluff to get to Elton John. Here, by the sound of it, arranger Paul Buckmaster's rather pompous orchestra was spliced in as an afterthought to flesh out music that had sufficient muscle to begin with, their choirs and Moogs and strings threaten to obscure Elton's voice and piano, everywhere that they appear at least momentarily diverting the listener's attention therefrom. Those acquainted with producer Gus Dudgeon's brilliant work with the Bonzos have ample reason to be mightily disillusioned with the good fellow for the excesses he allowed to run rampant here.

"But don't be scared away, for so immense a talent is Elton's that he'll delight you senseless despite it all. He's equally effective belting gospely rock and roll raves like 'Take Me To The Pilot' and the already much-covered 'Border Song' (neither of which one can resist leaping up heatedly to boogie to) in a tuneful snarl and intoning pretty McCartney-esque ballads like 'Your Song,' 'I Need You To Turn To,' or 'First Episode at Hienton' in a warm, intimate and wonderfully sympathetic tenor... And the orchestra was needed on neither 'Sixty Years On' nor 'The King Must Die,' for on both his voice creates sufficient drama on its own.

"A few warranted words on the album's words, by Bernie Taupin. At this hopefully early stage. in his evolution, Bernie all too often opts for the consciously poetic/arty where the straightforward would do better, tends to wander metaphorically, forces himself into some perfectly dreadful rhymes, occasionally employs ambiguity for its own sake, and generally seems intent on reproducing most of Keith Reid's early faults, the result being that one often has to consciously ignore the lyrics if he's to enjoy the song. He's definitely his most bearable when, as in 'The Greatest Discovery' or 'Hienton,' he's too busy narrating specific emotions and experiences for us to think about concealing his sentimentality with poetistic tricks. Rock and roll has too few unabashed sentimentalists writing songs as it is: let it all hang out, Bernie."

"Everyone said how brilliant it was. No one could talk about anything else." ~Sue Ayton, DJM

The album received a Grammy nomination for Album of the Year. It is also in the Grammy Hall of Fame.

The album is #468 on *Rolling Stone*'s list of The 500 Greatest Albums of All Time.

What Elton Said

Elton: "We'd started writing a different class of song. We grew up."

Factoids

The budget for the album was a mere £6,000; but so determined were Dudgeon and Buckmaster to make the album an orchestral feast that they managed to squeeze another £1,500 out of Dick James. In the end, the total expenditure came close to £10,000.

So generous is *Elton John* with its renewable treasures that Elton's *Live in Australia with the Melbourne Symphony Orchestra* album, recorded 17 years later, includes no less than seven of its 10 tracks.

On the week the album hit the stores, the Beatles broke up.

Your Song

Written by	Elton John, Bernie Taupin
Chart position	#8 (US Billboard Hot 100) / #7 (UK Singles Chart)
Released	10/26/1970
B-side	"Take Me to the Pilot" / "Into the Old Man's Shoes"
From the album	*Goodbye Yellow Brick Road*

Session [at] De Lane Lea [Studio]. Bobby Bruce. Stayed home today. Went to South Harrow market. The session was hilarious. Didn't do anything in the end. Wrote 'Your Song'.

~Elton's diary

For almost everyone, this song is where Elton John begins.

It's also the moment, in the film *Rocketman*, when the Elton/Bernie partnership truly emerges. The scene in the film shows Bernie and Elton in the home of Elton's mother, with Bernie upstairs in the bathroom and Elton downstairs at the piano. He selects "Your Song" from Bernie's latest stack of lyrics and begins noodling away at a melody, half-singing as he goes. Within a moment or two he has the song, and begins singing and playing it in earnest. Bernie, astonished at what he's hearing, descends the stairs to listen more closely, and Elton's mother and grandmother slip into the room to listen as well. While fictionalized, that depiction isn't far from the truth.

"Your Song", from his second album Elton John, introduced him to the world. But his first hit was completely accidental: released in October 1970, it was actually the B-side of the intended single, "Take Me to the Pilot", which Elton's management felt was a much more commercial tune. The disc jockeys of the world disagreed, playing "Your Song" instead – and making it a Top 10 hit in both the US and UK.

The song paved the way for the great singer/songwriters of the early Seventies – Cat Stevens, Carole King, James Taylor, Don McLean – by demonstrating how receptive the radio listener could be to simple, vulnerable songs, sung gently with soft accompaniment.

"'Your Song' was the first hit for Elton and Bernie, and the first to be universally accepted as evidence of their songwriting talent. Writing it, seeing it blossom into a hit, and savoring its growth and maturation over time was like watching the birth of a child and its flowering into a distinct human being over many years. Elton and Bernie had had many such children." ~Rock journalist Elizabeth J. Rosenthal

The Writing

Unlike most Elton/Bernie collaborations, "Your Song" was written long before Elton saw it, when Bernie was 17 ("...hence the extraordinary virginal sentiments," he said).

"The original lyric was written very rapidly on the kitchen table of Elton's mother's apartment in Northwood Hills in the suburbs of London, if I recall, on a particularly grubby piece of exercise paper," he said. More specifically, he wrote it "breakfast time sometime in 1969."

The Music

Elton: "It was written in five minutes, recorded in two."

The Recording

The demo of the song[5] so impressed both Gus Dudgeon and Paul Buckmaster that they both signed on to work with Elton as producer and arranger. "'Your Song' was the first thing I'd heard," Buckmaster said, "and it immediately locked me into wanting to do this record [*Elton John*]."

For the album version, Elton did the vocal and piano; three guitars were used, played by Frank Clark, Colin Green and Clive Hicks (whose

---

[5] The demo is included in EJ's 1990 box set *To Be Continued.*

guitar was a 12-string). The rhythm section included Barry Morgan on drums and Dave Richmond on bass.

The Response

"Your Song" is #137 of *Rolling Stone*'s list of The 500 Greatest Songs of All Time.

"The song itself is glowing and strangely haunting, the scoring is smooth and delicate and the performance is symptomatic of a new era of pop idols." ~Derek Johnson, *NME*

John Lennon heard the song, was deeply impressed by it, and befriended Elton: "I remember hearing Elton John's 'Your Song', heard it in America – it was one of Elton's first big hits – and remember thinking, 'Great, that's the first new thing that's happened since we [the Beatles] happened.' It was a step forward. There was something about his vocal that was an improvement on all of the English vocals until then. I was pleased with it." *Rolling Stone* agreed, as John Mendelsohn declared the song a "pretty McCartney-esque ballad."

When Elton and Bernie toured the US, Three Dog Night's Danny Hutton showed them Los Angeles, and took them to visit Brian Wilson of the Beach Boys. "I'll never forget arriving at Brian Wilson's house," Bernie said. "Danny Hutton rang at this big security gate and said, 'I've got Elton John and Bernie Taupin here.' Suddenly a voice on the intercom started singing, *'I hope you don't mind... I hope you don't mind...'* It was Brian Wilson, singing 'Your Song'."

British pop artist Nik Kershaw, who sat in on the *Ice on Fire* sessions in 1985, said, "[Elton] doesn't believe me, but the first record I ever bought was 'Your Song'. So he's always been a hero of mine."

It was inducted into the Grammy Hall of Fame in 1998.

What Elton/Bernie Said

Elton: "I don't think I've written a love song as good since." He has called it "a perfect song."

Bernie: "It's like the perennial ballad 'Your Song,' which has got to be one of the most naïve and childish lyrics in the entire repertoire of music, but I think the reason it still stands up is because it was real at the time. That was exactly what I was feeling. I was 17 years old and it was coming from someone whose outlook on love or experience with love was totally new and naïve."

Elton: "I've always said that number sounds like a song about a seventeen-year-old guy who is desperate to get laid. Which, at the time, it was."

"Now I could never write that song again or emulate it because the songs I write now that talk about love coming from people my age usually deal with broken marriages and where the children go. You have to write from where you are at a particular point in time, and 'Your Song' is exactly where I was coming from back then."

Elton: "I always thought 'Your Song' was written about one of his girlfriends, and when I asked him that, he just said, 'No it wasn't!' He gets fairly defensive."

Bernie: "This one is the one I recall like it was yesterday. The rest of them I'm a little shaky on. In retrospect, and I've said it on several occasions, I see this song as a bookend and its counterpart would be a song like 'Sacrifice.' 'Your Song' being a song about absolute naiveté in love while 'Sacrifice' is the complete opposite, the story of someone who's seen and done it all, as far as love's concerned, and come out the other end scarred but realistic about certain aspects of the real world."

Bernie: "I think 'Your Song' is a gem. Our classic, I'm not sure. I'll let others decide that. But it's like an old friend, it means so many things on equally as many levels. It's certainly proved its worth, and I've heard it sung a million times. It's like a good dog, it's always there."

Notable Covers

Three Dog Night covered "Your Song" on their 1970 album *It Ain't Easy*, which actually came out a month ahead of the *Elton John* album[6].

Soul singer Billy Paul did a version that he put on the flip side of his hit single "Me and Mrs. Jones".

Ellie Goulding put a version of it out as a single in 2010; it went to #2 on the UK Singles Chart.

Rod Stewart covered it on the tribute album *Two Rooms: Celebrating the Songs of Elton John & Bernie Taupin*.

Lady Gaga did a cover of it on *Revamp: Reimagining the Songs of Elton John & Bernie Taupin. Rolling Stone* praised Gaga's interpretation, saying she "uses the track's piano-led instrumentation as a vessel to set off her own vocal fireworks." She and Elton had previously done the song at the 2010 Grammies.

Ewan McGregor performed it in the musical film *Moulin Rouge!* in 2001.

The Hollies wanted to cover it, but didn't: "We knew Reg because he was a staff writer with a music publisher we used," Hollie guitarist Tony Hicks told *The Daily Mail* in 2013. "He was writing songs well before he became famous. One was 'Your Song'. I thought it would be a good one for the Hollies, and asked the publisher for permission to record it. He told me Elton had recorded it himself and it was due to be released in the US. He said, 'But it probably won't happen for him, so wait until it's all over.'"

Hollie Bobby Elliot told another version: "Tony Hicks and I went in to Uncle Dick – that's Dick James – and said that we'd like to do 'Your Song'. He said, 'No, I'm thinking of putting an orchestra on it, and it'll put Elton on the scene.' The fact that the Hollies wanted to do it helped Dick realize what a good artist Elton was. We missed having it, but it shows we could spot a good song."

---

[6] Elton had been opening for TDN at the time.

Factoids

So important was "Your Song" in the story of Elton and Bernie that they actually wrote a song about the writing of it - "We All Fall in Love Sometimes", which appeared on the autobiographical *Captain Fantastic and The Brown Dirt Cowboy.*

Elton performed the song at the Concert for Diana on July 1, 2007. The song was a favorite of Princess Diana's, and Elton said a number of times that the line "Yours are the sweetest eyes I've ever seen" made him think of her.

Elton also did a version with Italian tenor Alessandro Safina in 2002. That version went to #4 on the UK Singles Chart, outperforming the original.

"Your Song" was what Elton performed in his first-ever television appearance, on *The Andy Williams Show.*

Elton performed the song as part of his *Live in Australia with the Melbourne Symphony Orchestra* set.

In performing the song for the Queen Mother in a command performance at the Royal Lodge, Windsor, replacing the words "I'd buy a big house where we both could live" with "I'd buy Windsor Castle, Your Majesty".

On tour with Billy Joel in 1998, Elton would hand off "Your Song" to Joel, while he would cover "Uptown Girl".

It appears in an episode of "The Simpsons".

The running time is 4:03.

Tumbleweed Connection

Produced by	Gus Dudgeon
Engineered by	Robin Geoffrey Cable
Performed by	Elton John (vocals, piano, Hammond organ) Nigel Olsson (drums, vocals) Dee Murray (bass, vocals) Brian Dee (Hammond organ) Caleb Quaye (electric/acoustic guitars) Les Thatcher (acoustic guitar, 12-string guitar) Gordon Huntley (steel guitar) Mike Egan (acoustic guitar) Lesley Duncan (acoustic guitar, vocals) Herbie Flowers (bass) Dave Glover (bass) Chris Laurence (bass) Barry Morgan (drums) Roger Pope (drums) Robin Jones (congas, tambourine) Skaila Kanga (harp) Ian Duck (harmonica) Johnny Van Derek (violin) Karl Jenkins (oboe) Dusty Springfield, Madeline Bell, Heather Wheatman, Yvonne Wheatman, Kay Garner, Tony Hazzard, Tony Burrows, Tammi Hun (backing vocals)
Released	10/30/1970
Chart Position	#5 (US Billboard 200) / #2 (UK Albums Chart)
Sales	Platinum

After the relative success of *Elton John*, Bernie and Elton were feeling emboldened. The next album would be a concept album – still a new thing in pop/rock - and the tone would be country, the themes build around Americana and an earlier time.

This choice of themes represented an indulgence of Bernie's boyhood obsessions – cowboys, America, fathers and sons – and turned out to be a good one, foreshadowing a similar fascination evident in the upcoming work of the Eagles. Elton's music, pushed in a new direction, worked wonderfully.

The album wasn't particularly commercial – no singles were released in either the US or UK – but it demonstrated that Elton and Bernie were capable of generating more than just interesting pop songs.

Tracks

Side One
> **Ballad of a Well-Known Gun** (EJ/Taupin) - 4:59
> **Come Down in Time** (EJ/Taupin) - 3:25
> **Country Comfort** (EJ/Taupin) - 5:06
> **Son of Your Father** (EJ/Taupin) - 3:48�
> **My Father's Gun** (EJ/Taupin) - 6:20�

Side Two
> **Where to Now St. Peter?** (EJ/Taupin) - 4:11
> **Love Song** (Lesley Duncan) - 3:41
> **Amoreena** (EJ/Taupin) - 5:00
> **Talking Old Soldiers** (EJ/Taupin) - 4:06
> **Burn Down the Mission** (EJ/Taupin) - 6:22

The Writing

Soldiers and gunslingers populate several of Bernie's songs, including "Ballad of a Well-Known Gun", "Son of Your Father", "My Father's Gun" and "Where to Now, St. Peter?", inspired by the Civil War and the general violent cacophony of the Old West. The rural nineteenth century is the setting for "Country Comfort", "Amoreena" and "Talking Old Soldiers".

"Come Down in Time" has nothing to do with the Old West; it's a wistful song about disconnected lovers. And while "Burn Down the Mission", the album's best track, conveys imagery consistent with the rest of the album, its subtext – social revolution – is more abstract, an agitated essay on class struggle.

Among the songs in Bernie's stack was one that didn't fit the overall theme: "Madman Across the Water", an exploration of psychopathy narrated from the inside. It's hard to imagine where such a song would fit on *Tumbleweed*, but the point was moot: "Madman" didn't make the cut, not because of its incongruity, but because it didn't sound right. It was held over for the next album, and ended up being the title cut.

Finally, there was a track not written by Elton and Bernie – the first such occurrence on an Elton record. Lesley Duncan, who sang backing vocals on four tracks, contributed "Love Song" to Side Two, playing acoustic guitar on her own song.

The Music

Beyond Elton's synchronicity with Bernie's themes, he was at that time a big fan of The Band, a country rock outfit whose sound served as a general blueprint for the direction *Tumbleweed* would take, in tone if not implementation.

The music is dramatic – often melodramatic – and has its hooks in the nineteenth century West, from the brilliantly-integrated gospel voicings and New Orleans honky-tonk of "My Father's Son" to the mob-rumble undertones of the deceptively bright "Burn Down the Mission". That song, too, sounds gospel-ish, which along with its ascending key changes underscores the ironies of its inhabitants' rage: the God-fearing rally in righteous rapture as they set fire to the edifice of their subjugation.

The Recording

Pursuant of Bernie's vision, Gus populated the sessions with all the appropriate accoutrements: four acoustic guitarists; a 12-string guitar; a steel guitar, a violin, a harmonica.

"We'd all been listening to The Band at that point," said pedal-steel guitarist B.J. Cole. "For musicians in the early Seventies, The Band were probably our biggest influence at the time. They had a line to the American myth in the fact that Levon Helm came from the South, yet the rest were all Canadian guys who were just living the American myth. They had a similar approach to it as English musicians. They were observers in a way, so they got to it more effectively than people like the blues or country artists who were American and rather took it all for granted."

There were, however, some odd choices sprinkled atop the country-esque: "Come Down in Time", already a departure from the nostalgic themes, backed Elton's vocal with harp and oboe; and "Love Song" is likewise sparse and piano-free, as Elton sings with Lesley Duncan to her acoustic guitar. Both songs put the lie to critical accusations that Gus Dudgeon just couldn't restrain himself from over-producing.

Nigel and Dee, at this point the only other members of Elton's touring group, were both used in the sessions – together for the first time – but only on one track, "Amoreena". Gus Dudgeon didn't feel they were up to the standards his studio musicians (some of which were from the band Hookfoot) could be counted on to achieve. Nigel had made one appearance on *Empty Sky*; Dee had never played on an Elton record before.

The early take of "Madman" featured Mick Ronson on guitar, and while his part was energetic and competent, it didn't fit the mood of the song. It was for this reason that the song was kept off the album, and re-recorded with Davey Johnstone on guitar when the next album was recorded.

Critical Response

Jon Landau of *Rolling Stone* had this to say: "*Tumbleweed Connection* is interesting primarily because of the themes that Taupin has taken on and the melodies John has created. The performances are fine but somehow they lose the force one can envision them having had in some earlier stage of production. It is still an exciting album, one that I have played endlessly for a week, but it is also something of a missed opportunity. *Tumbleweed Connection* is simpler than John's last album and next time around I hope he goes all the way and gets down to nothing but the basics. He is one of the few who is good enough not to need anything else."

Robert Hilburn of the *LA Times* called *Tumbleweed* "that near-perfect album that artists often spend a whole career trying to produce." *Rolling Stone* lists *Tumbleweed Connection* as #463 on The 500 Greatest Albums of All Time.

What Bernie Said

Bernie: "It all began with watching TV as a kid. It stemmed from very plastic things like The Lone Ranger. I started reading about it then and I now have shelves of books on the subject.

Bernie: "I think we captured the atmosphere very well on *Tumbleweed Connection* – without name-dropping, Robbie Robertson thought it was great! It seems that people accept it much more in the States."

Factoids

The track "Country Comfort" was released as a single – but only in New Zealand. Rod Stewart covered the song on his second album, *Gasoline Alley*, in 1970. Keith Urban covered it on his 2004 album *Be Here*.

Amoreena is the name of Ray Williams' daughter, who is Elton's goddaughter.

Madman across the Water

Produced by	Gus Dudgeon
Engineered by	Robin Geoffrey Cable, Ken Scott
Performed by	Elton John (vocals, piano) Davey Johnstone (acoustic guitar, sitar, mandolin Nigel Olsson (drums, vocals) Dee Murray (bass, vocals) Ray Cooper (percussion, tambourine) Caleb Quaye (electric/acoustic guitars) B.J. Cole (steel guitar) Chris Spedding (electric guitar, slide guitar) David Glover (bass) Herbie Flowers (bass) Brian Odgers (bass) Chris Laurence (double bass) Roger Pope (drums) Terry Cox (drums) Barry Morgan (drums) Brian Dee (harmonium) Rick Wakeman (Hammond organ) Jack Emblow (accordion) Diana Lewis (ARP synthesizer) Lesley Duncan, Tony Burrows, Terry Steele, Liza Strike, Roger Cook, Barry St. John, Sue & Sunny (backing vocals)
Released	11/5/1971
Chart Position	#8 (US Billboard 200) / #41 (UK Albums Chart)
Sales	2x Platinum
Singles	"Levon" "Tiny Dancer"

Elton's fourth studio album was also his third in 1971, a testimony to the break-neck pace he and the band and the studio team were maintaining. Like its two immediate predecessors, *Elton John* and *Tumbleweed Connection*, it featured a seeming cast of thousands, a long proliferation of credits that included no less than five keyboard players (including Elton), four guitarists, five bass players, four drummers, 10 backing vocalists, and the Cantores em Ecclesia Choir.

That said, the ended Elton's session player era – for the Seventies, anyway. The reliance upon studio musicians to carry most of the water reflected Gus Dudgeon's lack of confidence in Elton's touring band – Dee and Nigel – as studio musicians. *Madman* was the last such album; Dee and Nigel, along with Davey, would be full partners, moving forward[7].

It was also Elton's most experimental album, then or since. It featured soaring orchestration by Paul Buckmaster, creating dark, majestic aural backdrops for Bernie's stark, cynical words. The album marks a new plateau for Bernie's work, demonstrating that touring – and the US, in particular – had expanded his horizons and packed away some of his naivete.

Davey Johnstone, Elton's most loyal and long-standing lieutenant, came aboard on *Madman* and would remain forever. In addition to Davey, *Madman* also marked the first appearance of percussionist Ray Cooper, who joined the band formally two years later – and, like Davey, remains with Elton to this day.

Tracks

Side One
        Tiny Dancer (EJ/Taupin) - 6:15
        Levon (EJ/Taupin) - 5:22

        Razor Face (EJ/Taupin) - 4:44
        Madman Across the Water (EJ/Taupin) - 5:56

Side Two
        Indian Sunset (EJ/Taupin) - 6:45
        Holiday Inn (EJ/Taupin) - 4:17
        Rotten Peaches (EJ/Taupin) - 4:56
        All the Nasties (EJ/Taupin) - 5:08
        Goodbye (EJ/Taupin) - 1:48

---

[7] Notably, two of the musicians from the *Madman* sessions – guitarist Caleb Quaye and drummer Roger Pope – would join the band four years later, following the firing of Dee and Nigel (see "Breaking Up the Band", page 144).

The Writing

Bernie's themes, both personal and abstract, showed greater depth than any previous album. His stack of lyrics sheets contained dark pages, intimate pages, and some excellent character portraiture.

"Tiny Dancer" was his paean to Maxine Feibelman, his new wife, and is brilliant just for the evocative tone it sets; but it also launches what follows as lessons-from-the-road, a biographical snapshot of the band's US tour ("Holiday Inn", "All the Nasties").

As usual, Bernie dives into the minds of an assortment of characters: the lonely, restless Levon Tostig, son of Alvin; the psychotic protagonist of the title track; a Native American warrior, ordered to stand down; an ex-addict who finds Jesus on the lam. And through it all, there was the palpable thread of Americana permeating each story.

"Back in the seventies, when people were saying that 'Madman across the Water' was about Richard Nixon, I thought, That is genius," Bernie said later. "I could never have thought of that."

Elton edited the lyrics on "Holiday Inn", as he would again on "Daniel".

The Music

Elton got excellent support from his session legions, but the music itself was brilliant. He'd never been better on the piano.

"[The piano intro of 'Levon' is] enough, all by itself, to guarantee immortality to the song," said critic Thomas Ryan, going on to say that 'Levon' "contains some of the most hauntingly beautiful evocative piano chords ever recorded."

Beyond the magnificent piano parts and lush, atmospheric arrangements that Paul Buckmaster provided, Elton made extensive use of symphonic structures, breaking songs into distinct sections, each with its own feel: from the staccato pulses in "Tiny Dancer" to the interludes in "Indian Sunset", the music is elegant, complex and sophisticated.

The title track itself is positively progressive, with a King Crimson-like hook figure connecting verse and chorus, an acoustic foundation anchoring the song as it fades and resurges, underscoring the instability of the protagonist; it is sonata-like in its building and rebuilding of the main theme, with an unpredictable variety in the development that disturbingly conveys his insanity.

There's a sense in all of this that Elton is trying to prove something; and, as it happened, that turned out to be true.

The Recording

Between the session players, the orchestra and the choir, Trident Studios were a madhouse. Despite this, the album was recorded in a mere four days – one day in February, three days in August. Gus Dudgeon remembered the sessions with great satisfaction:

"When you finally got into the studio, all of a sudden you would hear this orchestra running through the parts, and you could actually hear it being played by twenty or thirty people," he said. "I would be thinking, wow, this is just magic, because that would be the first time anybody had actually heard it. Then you would finally marry the string parts up with the orchestra and it was such a buzz. It was a white-knuckle ride. There's nothing like hearing an orchestra play a great arrangement."

The album's title track had actually been recorded during the *Tumbleweed Connection* sessions and had turned out very differently. Mick Ronson had played the guitar, and it had been blistering, very different from the acoustic riff Davey had come up with. Though Ronson had done a fine job, the feeling was that the song needed to go in a different direction, and was thus shelved.

As astounding as "Madman" turned out to be, "Tiny Dancer" is the album's true gem, with "Levon" a close second (it is, on balance, one of the finest Side Ones of Elton's career). A signature slide guitar part was used to link bridge to chorus, played by B.J. Cole; the punchy staccato of Elton's piano chords in the connecting phrase signaled his sophisticated approach to the song structures to follow; and the song was Elton's first significant use of falsetto voice in the studio.

Nigel and Dee were only used on one track - "All the Nasties". Davey, on the other hand, brought in to fix "Madman", was asked to play acoustic guitar parts on "Tiny Dancer" and "Holiday Inn", and to add mandolin and sitar to "Indian Sunset".

It would be their last album recorded at Trident. The next would be done at Château d'Hérouville, where they would remain through *Goodbye Yellow Brick Road*.

Critical Response

Madman performed poorly in the UK, compared to Elton's previous albums. It never rose above #41, and spent only two weeks on the charts. It did better in the US, rising to #8 and going Gold a month later. Neither of the singles - "Tiny Dancer" and "Levon" - cracked the Top 20; on the other hand, in the UK, DJM didn't bother to release any singles at all.

Alec Dubro, *Rolling Stone*: "A record with a theme, it's an account, sometimes photographic, sometimes emotional, all too often metaphorical, of Elton John in America — the madman across the water... *Madman* won't really crush any John fans, for he sings with the same power and brilliance he's shown since he broke. But, it probably won't draw any either. *Madman* is a difficult, sometimes impossibly dense record. America is worthy of a better story than this record and Elton John needs a better story than this to sing."

"Two tracks stand out for their utter, wonderful uncommerciality in any age. One is 'Levon', Bernie Taupin's own 'A Day in the Life', about a man born 'on the day the New York Times said 'God is dead.' The other is 'Madman Across the Water' itself, soliloquy of a lunatic on visiting day, played by an orchestra schizophrenically uncertain whether it is funeral dirge or slow-motion funk." ~Biographer Philip Norman

What Elton/Bernie Said

Elton: "I still like that album, but really Bernie and I had hit a very odd situation when we came to cut it. We had written only about eight songs that year, working on them separately, and it came to the point that there was nothing to fall back on if we'd hated one of the tracks. Normally we write about 25 numbers a year so you can tell the sort of state we were in. So *Madman* wrapped up the tail end of our writing, and it was the very last album of its kind we'll ever do."

Elton has said that the song on the album he feels most connected to is the title track.

Because of the album's poor performance, "I thought of quitting," Elton said. "I really thought I'd gone as far as I was going to."

Bernie: "What that album still reminds me of most is simply being in America, driving down the freeways in LA, listening to the car radio."

Factoids

The album cover shows a denim pocket with the title and Elton's name hand-embroidered; no picture of Elton was used. Its designer insisted it be done by hand, rather than created in a photo lab, adding time and expense to the completion of the album art, which caused some acrimony.

Of the albums released in The Classic Years series, *Madman* was the first not to include any bonus tracks. There was, however, a track that could have been included: "Rock Me When I'm Gone", which Elton and Bernie had written for Long John Baldry, who had recorded it. It appears on the *Rare Masters* compilation.

A wonderful live version of "Madman" can be found on *Live in Australia with the Melbourne Symphony Orchestra*, with the orchestra earnestly interpreting Paul Buckmaster's frenetic score. Bruce Hornsby, a piano stylist in Elton's own tradition, covered it on *Two Rooms*.

Rick Wakeman, keyboardist for the progressive powerhouse Yes, played Hammond organ on "Razor Face", "Madman", and "Holiday Inn".

Blue Jean Baby

The songwriting partnership of Elton John and Bernie Taupin may be second only to Lennon/McCartney among 20th century collaborations. It produced a vast list of hit songs, from "Goodbye Yellow Brick Road" to "Daniel" to "Candle in the Wind" to "Bennie and the Jets" to "Crocodile Rock", naming only a handful, across more than four decades.

Their songwriting method is legend: Bernie would, alone in a room, generate a pile of lyrics. He would turn them over to Elton who, alone in a room with a piano, would turn them into songs. From that simple method has arisen more than 35 albums and 300 hundred million records sold.

One of those early songs made it to Taupin's pen all the way from Los Angeles – a seamstress named Maxine Feibelman, who joined Elton's 1970 tour and quickly became the object of Taupin's affections. He married her the following year, with Elton standing as best man.

Thus "Tiny Dancer", from the album *Madman Across the Water*, became Elton's fifth single, following "Take Me to the Pilot", "Your Song", "Friends" and "Levon", and immediately preceding "Rocket Man". It stalled at #41, far below many of his other hits, and so was not as immediately well-known.

That changed over the years, as it became a late-blooming classic in the Elton canon, prominent in Cameron Crowe's *Almost Famous* and taking its place on the 1992 *Greatest Hits Vol. II* redux.

Maxine, then, actually lived the song "Tiny Dancer" - touring with Taupin, whom she continued to inspire, and Elton, whose stompy fits and tantrums soon wore thin for her. On one such occasion, when Elton began to rant, she turned to her husband:

"Uh, oh," she said, "The bitch is back..."

Tiny Dancer

Written by	Elton John, Bernie Taupin
Chart position	#41 (US Billboard Hot 100) / #70 (UK Singles Chart)
Released	2/4/1974
B-side	"Razor Face"
From the album	*Madman Across the Water*

Almost Famous, Cameron Crowe's 2000 love letter to early-Seventies rock, is a joy. It's a fictionalized version of his own entry into the rock ecosphere, the chronicle of a teenage journalist shadowing an up-and-coming rock band. The emotional apex of the film is a moment when the band and the teenager and his would-be girlfriend are on the open highway in the tour bus, and Elton's "Tiny Dancer" pops up on the radio, and everyone surrenders to the joy of the song, singing along – recalling the experience of millions of early-Seventies teens, on school buses across the US. The scene is particularly poignant because at this point in the movie, the band all want to kill each other – but "Tiny Dancer" reunites them through their love of music[8]:

"Cameron Crowe made it the highlight of *Almost Famous*, his autobiographical account of hitting the road as a young *Rolling Stone* writer. He's on the tour bus with the band, but he's a total outsider in this scene, not to mention a kid. The band guys sit in stony silence, pissed at each other, until the Elton John song on the radio coaxes them to sing along. Golden-goddess groupie queen Penny Lane leads the chorus. The drummer taps his sticks on the vinyl bus seat. Harmony is restored. Penny tells the boy that he's home, and he realizes that she's right."

That's "Tiny Dancer" - pure joy. It didn't soar all that high on first release (it barely missed the Top 40 in the US) - but it caught up later; like "Levon", the track that follows it on *Madman Across the Water*, it was a late bloomer.

---

[8] *Rolling Stone* rated this scene #11 among its 30 Greatest Rock and Roll Movie Moments.

The Writing

There are conflicting versions of Bernie's inspiration. On the one hand, the lyrics perfectly describe his early time with his first wife, Maxine Feibelman[9]; Bernie confirmed this interpretation in a 1973 *Rolling Stone* interview.

On the other hand, Bernie said, "We came to California in the fall of 1970, and sunshine radiated from the populace. I was trying to capture the spirit of that time, encapsulated by the women we met - especially at the clothes stores up and down the Strip in LA. They were free spirits, sexy in hip-huggers and lacy blouses, and very ethereal, the way they moved. So different from what I'd been used to in England. And they all wanted to sew patches on your jeans. They'd mother you and sleep with you - it was the perfect Oedipal complex."

The Music

Elton structured the song in classical style, building it out in distinct sections that build upon one another. He would repeat this style forever more, even on the next track on *Madman* ("Levon"), and with astonishing complexity just two songs later ("Madman Across the Water", the closing track of the album side).

Elton: "Look at the words... As soon as you get to the word 'ballerina' you know it's not going to be fast. It's going to be gentle and sort of quite slow."[10]

The Recording

"Tiny Dancer" marks Elton's first significant use of falsetto – ascending into notes above the normal vocal register – which would become his trademark. Once he took this step, a number of other artists – most notably the Bee Gees – would make it a performance staple.

[9] See "Blue Jean Baby", page 49.

[10] For the archival video of this moment, in which Elton explains the song, google "Elton John Tiny Dancer 1970 interview."

Davey Johnstone, called into the *Madman* sessions to fix "Madman" itself, plays acoustic guitar on this track.

There are 10 backing vocalists on the track.

Though the song was released as a single in the US, it was released at its full album length – over six minutes, longer than "Bohemian Rhapsody". For this reason, it is believed, it was doomed as a high-ranking radio cut; its primary home was on FM.

The Response

Rolling Stone's Alec Dubro: "It has the delicate melody, virtuoso singing, and innovative arranging that have marked Elton John since 'Your Song.' In fact, it sounds like 'Your Song,' with maybe some other familiar melody and a few new touches like a pedal steel. But that's OK; it may be the same song, but it's a good song."

What Elton Said

Elton, re *Almost Famous*: "Jeffrey Katzenberg called me and said, 'There's a scene in this film which is going to make 'Tiny Dancer' a hit all over again.' When I saw it, I said, 'Oh my God!' I used to play 'Tiny Dancer' in England and it would go down like a lead zeppelin. Cameron resurrected that song." (After the run of the film, Elton re-integrated "Tiny Dancer" into his live show.)

Notable Covers

Ben Folds covered the song in his 2002 album *Ben Folds Live*. He released it as a promo single.

Country artist Tim McGraw did a version on 2002's *Tim McGraw and the Dancehall Doctors*, and he and Elton performed it together at the American Music Awards.

Florence and the Machine did a tribute version on 2018's *Revamp: Reimagining the Songs of Elton John & Bernie Taupin.*

Factoids

Elton performed the song with Miley Cyrus at the 2018 Grammy Awards, just before he announced the *Farewell Yellow Brick Road* tour.

The running time is 6:12.

Levon

Written by	Elton John, Bernie Taupin
Chart position	#24 (US Billboard Hot 100)
Released	11/29/1971
B-side	"Goodbye"
From the album	*Madman Across the Water*

The Writing

Elton: "It's about a guy who just gets bored doing the same thing. It's just somebody who gets bored with blowing up balloons and he just wants to get away from it but he can't because it's the family ritual."

Bernie told Rolling Stone that he really had no intended meaning for the lyrics. "It was a free-form writing," he said. "It was just lines that came out that were interesting."
He was inspired to name the song after Levon Helm, the drummer/singer and co-founder of The Band (The Band was Bernie and Elton's favorite band at the time the song was written). Beyond that, Bernie said, there is no other connection between Helm and the character in the song.

The Recording

Biographer Philip Norman called "Levon" Bernie Taupin's "A Day in the Life".

The orchestration on the track was done by Paul Buckmaster.

British pop singer Tony Burrows provided the backing vocals.

The Response

Released in the US but not in the UK, "Levon" cracked the Top 40 but only rose to #24. It out-performed "Tiny Dancer", the other single from *Madman Across the Water*, which only made it to #41. Elton's US distributer at the time, Uni, wanted to edit the single down for airplay, but Elton refused.

"Levon" stands out on the radio simply because any Elton John song would. But, here we begin to encounter a knotty problem that worsens as the album continues. i.e., what the hell is he talking about?"
~Alec Dubro, *Rolling Stone*

"Led by John's vocal melodies, 'Levon' beautifully builds throughout. Here, Taupin's obscure lyrics are much thought provoking and work better overall with the rich song craft. A fine acoustic accompanies the piano of the first verse while Brian Odger's funky bass line is accompanied by a cool honky-tonk piano during the second verse. Topping it all off are the orchestral strings, which are much more up front and assert their presence more here than anywhere else on the album. The long coda contains a blend of many of these styles executed in harmony, a real tribute to Dudgeon's production style." ~Rick Albano, *Classic Rock Review*

"[The piano intro of 'Levon' is] enough, all by itself, to guarantee immortality to the song," said critic Thomas Ryan, going on to say that 'Levon' "contains some of the most hauntingly beautiful evocative piano chords ever recorded."

Notable Covers

Jon Bon Jovi did a cover of "Levon" for the *Two Rooms* tribute album, and said that it is his favorite song of all time, saying also that Elton is his idol.

Myles Kennedy did his own version, with some altered lyrics, on SiriusXM Octane, also citing Elton as a childhood idol and musical influence.

Canadian singer-songwriter Billy Klippert released a cover as a single in 2004, from his self-titled debut album.

Mary McCreary covered it in 1974 on her album *Jezebel*.

Factoids

One of Elton's two sons is named Zachary Jackson Levon Furnish-John.

The *New York Times* actually said, on March 24, 1968, that "'God is Dead' Doctrine Losing Ground to 'Theology of Hope'".

The running time is 5:22.

At the Honky Château

The Honky Château - Château d'Hérouville, north of Paris, where Strawberry Studios existed in pastoral fields where sat a somewhat dilapidated villa – became not just a headquarters for the band, but a refuge. With Davey in the band, they were complete, and the château, an environment where they could live and bond, as well as record, made them a family.

The albums *Honky Château*, *Don't Shoot Me I'm Only the Piano Player*, and *Goodbye Yellow Brick Road* – all Elton classics – were born there.

From *Rolling Stone*:

"After the disastrous Jamaica sessions, Elton, Bernie, producer Gus Dudgeon, bassist Dee Murray, drummer Nigel Olsson and guitarist Davey Johnstone headed back to Château d'Hérouville, a 18th century château in northern France where they'd recorded their previous two albums, *Don't Shoot Me I'm Only the Piano Player* and *Honky Château*."

Elton: "When we got there, we really had to make up for lost time. I think that probably accelerated the writing process and the recording process even more."

Bernie: "There was definitely the comfort of retuning to a place that you really were familiar with. So we basically set up camp, and everything really went pretty swimmingly."

Elton: "During a typical day the band would come down, there'd be instruments around the breakfast table, Bernie would be writing at the typewriter, I'd be sitting at the electric piano, and as the band came down for breakfast, I would write the song, they would pick up their instruments and play it."

Bernie: "There was a piano in the corner of the dining room and there was a long communal table where all the guys used to sit and eat breakfast. Elton would come up with a tune during breakfast. I'd write my songs longhand. I'm pretty sure I didn't have a typewriter. One of the few things I remember very clearly, and this is easy to visualize now, is sitting on the side of my bed with a notepad, just writing. I'd just write stream-of-conscious lyrics."

Elton: "We'd record about three or four tracks a day. They were mostly made up on the day they were recorded. We were a very tight band with a lot of touring experience. We'd capture more songs in two or three takes. The whole record took about eighteen days."

Davey: "One half of the château was a studio, the other half was where we all lived. It was a residential area where we all slept and whatever, and had our meals. We'd wake up in the morning, go downstairs and there was a little bare-bones setup with a little amp and a couple of guitars, banjo, mandolin for me, Dee's bass amp, a small kit for Nigel and an electric piano for Elton. I'd come down and the guys would fall down one by one and we'd have some breakfast, have a baguette with a cup of coffee. We'd then immediately saunter over to the area where our instruments were and Elton would already be looking at lyrics and working out what he was gonna start with.

"We would then walk over to the studio, plug in and start running down these songs and recording them. That's just the way it would go. Day by day, we developed a way of working where nobody had to say anything to each other. Elton never said, "Well, how about you play this?" or "What about playing that?" He'd never tell me to play a part. It happened very rarely, very, very rarely, I think most famously on the *Yellow Brick Road* record, which we were cutting three, four songs a day in the studio. We'd just done "Candle in the Wind," the band version that's on the record. He said, "Davey, I've got this great idea for a guitar part," and he sang me the guitar part. I looked at him and I said, "Oh, no. Fuck me, that sounds a bit cheesy." I said, "I'll try it," obviously.

"They ran the song. When the part came up where he wanted me to play this guitar line, I played it, and it worked great. I kind of went, 'Okay, I've got to listen to this guy.' Although he can't play guitar, he obviously loves guitar. He kind of knows what he wants in certain areas. He really knows what he wants. We've continued to have this great relationship over the years about that."

Honky Château

Produced by	Gus Dudgeon
Engineered by	Ken Scott
Performed by	Elton John (vocals, piano, electric piano, Hammond organ, harmonium) Davey Johnstone (electric/acoustic guitars, slide guitar, steel guitar, banjo, mandolin, vocals) Dee Murray (bass, vocals) Nigel Olsson (drums, congas, tambourine, vocals) Ivan Julien (trumpet) Jacques Bolognesi (trombone) Jean-Louis Chautemps (saxophone) Alain Hatot (saxophone) Jean-Luc Ponty (electric violin) Larry Smith (tap dance) David Hentschel (ARP synthesizer) Ray Cooper (congas) Gus Dudgeon (whistle, backing vocals) Madeline Bell, Liza Strike, Larry Steel, Tony Hazzard (backing vocals)
Released	5/19/1972
Chart Position	#1 (US Billboard 200) / #2 (UK Albums Chart)
Sales	Platinum
Singles	"Rocket Man" "Honky Cat"

Elton's first US #1 album marked the beginning of a four-album residency at Château d'Hérouville in France, as well as the first album to feature Elton's touring band as his core studio team. This winning combination resulted in a string of six consecutive #1 albums in the US, through 1975's *Rock of the Westies*.

It wasn't the first truly eclectic album Elton had created, but it was most eclectic one he'd generated up to that point. The album continued the rock, country rock and balladry that were already well-established, but also took forays into soul and blues.

It made for an ideal welcome to new band member Davey Johnstone, who'd first appeared on the previous album's title track, given his versatility with stringed instruments. He contributed electric guitar, acoustic guitar, slide guitar, pedal-steel guitar, banjo and mandolin.

Along with all these changes came a new studio sensibility. The songs were shorter, the arrangements less complex.

"The decision had been made that *Madman across the Water* was the end of Chapter One," said engineer Ken Scott, "and that it was about time to move on and do something completely different, and that something different was *Honky Château.*"

Tracks

Side One
  Honky Cat (EJ/Taupin) - 5:13
  Mellow (EJ/Taupin) - 5:32
  I Think I'm Going to Kill Myself (EJ/Taupin) - 3:35
  Susie (Dramas) (EJ/Taupin) - 3:25
  Rocket Man (EJ/Taupin) - 4:45

Side Two
  Salvation (EJ/Taupin) - 3:58
  Slave (EJ/Taupin) - 4:22
  Amy (EJ/Taupin) - 4:03
  Mona Lisas and Mad Hatters (EJ/Taupin) - 5:00
  Hercules (EJ/Taupin) - 5:20

The Writing

Bernie's obsession with America, and its past in particular, had led to *Tumbleweed Connection*, which was more myth than reality. On *Château*, he took it further, examining slavery, urban life, youth culture, and the final frontier.

There's the usual assortment of interesting characters, from obsessed and pining teenagers to a jealous lover to an alienated astronaut; but Bernie himself is the "honky cat" and he threw in a second autobiographical gesture with "Mellow", a sex song, is about his idyllic life with his wife Maxine, the Tiny Dancer, in their pastoral new home, Piglet-in-the-Wilds.

One of his most sober lyrics in the batch, apart from "Rocket Man", is the haunting "Mona Lisas and Mad Hatters", perhaps the greatest Elton song you've never heard. The lyric was inspired by a shooting that occurred in the streets of New York below the hotel room Bernie was staying in, and serves as an indictment of the vast city's cold inhabitants.

The Music

Elton seemed anxious to get away from the darkness and bombast of Madman, writing spirited music for Bernie's mythologies. He pushed the jazz harder on "I Think I'm Going to Kill Myself", once again setting a tone that was the opposite of the lyric; he gave "Salvation" an authentic tent revival vibe; his honky-tonk New Orleans piano became a tying bind, used not only in "Honky Cat" but "Mellow" and "Hercules".

The Recording

Versatility was the theme in the studio. Each song was an empty canvas, waiting for something completely new. Davey, the newcomer, acquitted himself spectacularly, innovating with guitar-as-sound-effect in "Rocket Man"; building up the sound of the American South with stacked guitars and banjo on "Slave"; dressing "Mona Lisas and Mad Hatters" in gentle mandolin.

Dancer "Legs" Larry Smith does a jaunty little tap dance at the end of "I Think I'm Going to Kill Myself"; Ken Scott said he brought in his own tap floor.

On "Slave", Elton's vocal parodied Mick Jagger.

Critical Response

Rolling Stone's Jon Landau called *Honky Château* "a rich, warm, satisfying album that stands head and shoulders above the morass of current releases... Musically more varied, emotionally less contrived, lyrically more lucid than *Tumbleweed Connection, Château* rivals *Elton John* as his best work to date and evidences growth at every possible level... *Honky Château* is ultimately a solid work with enough happening to keep someone listening for weeks trying to absorb everything on it. And, as each additional layer is revealed to the listener, he is constantly reminded that this is one of the rare albums released this year worth pursuing at length, for it rewards each additional playing with increased enlightenment and enjoyment."

Stephen Thomas Erlewine at Allmusic.com wrote that the album "plays as the most focused and accomplished set of songs Elton John and Bernie Taupin ever wrote."

Rock journalist David Buckley, on "Mona Lisas and Mad Hatters": "Although by no means as well known as 'Your Song' and never released as an A-side single, it deserves to be thought of as one of Elton's classics. The paired-down arrangement with piano and mandolin but no drums gave the song a hymn-like effect. The lyric encapsulated Bernie's feelings on his first visit to New York; that sense of big a very small fish in a very big pond, where everything is more vivid and more different than expected."

What Elton/Bernie Said

Elton: "*Honky Château* was a really important album for us. We'd made it but we had one final bridge to cross, which was to make a great album."

Bernie: "It will shock a few people. I think we've gone as far as we can on the grand scale with string arrangements and that. We just want to get back to the roots."

Elton: "I was just about ready to give up [before *Honky Château*]... I got very depressed with all the bad reviews of *Madman*."

Elton: "[No one] can turn around and say, 'Oh, it's Elton and his bloody one-hundred-piece orchestra again."

Factoids

The final track, "Hercules", was intended as the album's third single, but that plan was abandoned. Elton legally changed his middle name to Hercules during the *Honky Château* sessions.

After the recording of *Honky Château*, Elton was so thrilled with what his band had accomplished that he offered them royalties. "That was unheard of," said Nigel. "It still is, to this day."

Rocket Man

Written by	Elton John, Bernie Taupin
Chart position	#6 (US Billboard Hot 100) / #2 (UK Singles Chart)
Released	3/2/1972
B-side	"Susie (Dramas)"
From the album	*Honky Château*

So central is "Rocket Man" to Elton's career that it became his nickname (hence the title of his biopic – *Rocketman*).

If we can call the period covering *Empty Sky* through *Madman Across the Water* (the first four studio albums) Phase I of Elton's career, then "Rocket Man" launched Phase II. It was the first single to feature the band – Elton, Davey, Nigel and Dee – as the core studio musicians; it was the first to feature Davey, Nigel and Dee as the backing vocal team. It was the first exemplar of what can be characterized as Elton's classic sound, continued on "Candle in the Wind", "Goodbye Yellow Brick Road", "Lucy in the Sky with Diamonds", "Someone Saved My Life Tonight" and others.

This phase of Elton's career would continue through *Don't Shoot Me I'm Only the Piano Player, Goodbye Yellow Brick Road,* and *Caribou,* and *Captain Fantastic and the Brown Dirt Cowboy* - ending just before *Rock of the Westies*, when Elton dismissed Nigel and Dee.

Like so many of Elton's songs, "Rocket Man" is a moving character study, simultaneously personal and abstract, with the title character's narration of his space journey emanating isolation and loneliness, as well as confessing his deep feelings for the family he is missing. The chorus, with its transcendent vocals, remains a steadfast concert sing-along.

The Writing

Bernie had more inspiration than usual on "Rocket Man". He freely acknowledged being inspired by David Bowie's "Space Oddity" (coincidentally, Gus Dudgeon produced both songs), and Bowie caught the similarities himself[11]. But Ray Bradbury's short story "The Rocket Man"[12] was likewise an inspiration, and other sources cite Bernie's sighting of a meteor and another song inspired by Bradbury - "Rocket Man" by Pearls Before Swine, written by Tom Rapp, from their 1970 album *The Use of Ashes* – as influences.

The Bradbury story and the Pearls Before Swine song tell similar stories. Bradbury's tale describes a child whose astronaut father has been ordered into space, and has mixed feelings about leaving his family; the PBS song continues that narrative, to the point of the child not being able to look at the stars after his father dies up there.

Rock journalist Elizabeth Rosenthal has noted that many thought the similarities between the Rocket Man character and Bowie's Major Tom to be intentional.

The first part of the song came to Bernie while he was driving to his parents' home, and he had nothing on hand with which to write it down, forcing himself to repeat the words over and over to himself so that he wouldn't forget them.

"The words just came into my head: 'She packed my bags last night, pre-flight. Zero hour is nine a.m.' I remember jumping out of my car and running into my parents' house, shouting, 'Please don't anyone talk to me until I've written this down.'"

The Music

"I saw Elton write 'Rocket Man' in ten minutes right in front of me," said engineer Ken Scott, recalling the *Honky Château* sessions. "Bernie would go up to his room after dinner every night around 9 p.m. He would come down the next day with several sheets of paper and give them to Elton. Elton would look at them and say, 'Oh, that one looks good,' and put it to one side and he'd keep going through them until he'd come up with two or three he really liked. Then he would go over

[11] When David Bowie died in 2016, Elton did a mash-up of the two songs in tribute.

[12] The story is found in Bradbury's short story collection *The Illustrated Man*.

to the piano and start working on them. The one that really stuck out was 'Rocket Man', because in just ten minutes it was there."

The Recording

As said above, "Rocket Man" was the first single recorded by the classic band, without session players (though engineer David Hentschel played the ARP synthesizer), and ushered in the exquisite sound of the soaring background vocals of Davey, Nigel and Dee.

Two stand-out sounds distinguish "Rocket Man" as unique in Elton's canon: Davey's brilliant upward-slide guitar work, metaphorically representing the launch of the spacecraft, and David Hentschel's work on the ARP synthesizer.

"Since I was the only person at Trident there with a formal music education, I was elected as the programmer/session player," he said. "Gus had heard a couple of my demos and was keen to use these news sounds - 'Rocket Man' was the perfect subject matter for this new space age technology."

The Response

When it peaked on the charts, "Rocket Man" was his highest ranking single up to that time, surpassing "Your Song". Its huge success pulled him out of the funk he'd inhabited since Madman had tanked, and gave both him and Gus Dudgeon a renewed confidence in the band.

"When 'Rocket Man' was on *Top of the Pops*, I think that was the turning point in Elton's career in England... I think, then, everyone started to notice Elton John." ~Linda Stacey, Elton John Fan Club

The song has been interpreted as a metaphor for the isolation rock stars feel on their stratospheric journeys, which cause them to become increasingly isolated, distanced from those they love.

What Bernie Said

Bernie: "Nobody but Elton could have sung that line from 'Rocket Man' about being high as a kite without getting banned from the radio."

Bernie, responding to an accusation that he'd ripped off David Bowie: "Oh no, we didn't steal that one from Bowie. We stole if from another bloke, called Tom Rapp."

Notable Covers

Kate Bush covered the song on the *Two Rooms* tribute album. Her version was released as a single, and went to #12 in the UK. Elton and Bernie granted her complete creative control, and she took the interesting approach of giving the song a reggae feel.

William Shatner's cover is by far the most horrendous, not just of "Rocket Man", but of just about any song, any time, anywhere. He did it live at the 1978 Science Fiction Film Awards[13], making it an accompanied reading, as with his covers of "Mr. Tambourine Man" and "Lucy in the Sky with Diamonds" from his 1968 album *The Transformed Man.*

Little Big Town covered the tune on the 2018 Elton tribute *Restoration.* Sounds from NASA's Mission Juno, a Jupiter probe, were used in the recording.

Elton performed the song at the launch of the Space Shuttle *Discovery* in 1998.

When Elton played the Soviet Union in 1979, the song title "Rocket Man" was replaced in the concert program with "Cosmonaut".

---

[13] Bernie Taupin introduced him that night.

Factoids

"Rocket Man" is #245 on *Rolling Stone*'s list of The 500 Greatest Songs of All Time.

While in Houston during the 1972 US tour, Elton asked for and received permission to visit the NASA space center. He and the band spent four hours there, had lunch with *Apollo 15* pilot Al Worden, got to try out the Apollo flight simulator, and watched the splashdown of *Apollo 16*.

Elton named his record company Rocket Records.

His 2012 anthology is called *Rocket Man: The Definitive Hits*.

Donald Trump uses the name "Rocket Man" as a derogatory reference to North Korean leader Kim Jong Un. The moniker is not original with Trump; *The Economist* called Kim Jong II, his father, "The Rocket Man" in a 2006 issue.

Bernie Taupin has publicly disapproved of Trump's use of the nickname, telling the *Wall Street Journal*, "The context bothered me. The thought that World War III could start over the use of my song title was disturbing. I also was uncomfortable that something of mine that was culturally iconic could be used in such a way. But what could I do? Sue him for cultural appropriation? As a songwriter, you're powerless to stop something like that. However, if the use of 'Rocket Man' results in peace, I will be very happy to take full credit for it."

The running time is 4:41.

Honky Cat

Written by	Elton John, Bernie Taupin
Chart position	#8 (US Billboard Hot 100) / #31 (UK Singles Chart)
Released	7/31/1972
B-sides	"Slave"
From the album	*Honky Château*

Elton's third Top 10 single (and the second from Honky Château) was recorded at the Château d'Hérouville in France, as was "Rocket Man". The studio at the château, which included living quarters and was surrounded by pastoral grounds, would remain the band's studio headquarters through *Goodbye Yellow Brick Road.* So quickly did the band take to their new home that they named it – and the album – after this song.

With its elaborate horns and syncopated feel, the song both veers away from Elton's rock and ballad modes and captures a new energy, expanding his stylistic range.

The Writing

The "honky cat" is Bernie himself, writing another of many lyrics expressing his rural nature and his desire to steer clear of city life.

The Music

Elton went pure Dixieland in conceiving the music, intent on setting up Bernie's wide-eyed-country-boy with a bright-lights, big-city feel. Once again, Bernie's dead-serious lyric is housed within Elton's disarming counter-mood, setting up an irony.

The Recording

The contrast between the Honky Cat's two worlds is perfectly framed by Gus, handing Davey a banjo to capture the character's country rube quality while surrounding him with jazzy horns, signifying New Orleans.

The Response

"Honky Cat" did well in the US, poorly in the UK, a pattern that plagued Elton constantly in the early Seventies.

Notable Covers

Lee Ann Womack covered "Honky Cat" on the 2018 tribute album *Restoration: Reimagining the Songs of Elton John & Bernie Taupin.*

Factoids

There's a live version of the song on the album *Here and There.*

The running time of the edited single is 4:07, considerably shorter than the album version, 5:13.

Don't Shoot Me I'm Only the Piano Player

Produced by	Gus Dudgeon
Engineered by	Ken Scott
Performed by	Elton John (vocals, piano, electric piano, organ, harmonium, mellotron) Davey Johnstone (electric/acoustic guitars, banjo, sitar, mandolin, vocals Nigel Olsson (drums, percussion, vocals) Dee Murray (bass, vocals) Jean-Louis Bolognesi (saxophone) Ken Scott (ARP synthesizer) Ivan Jullien (trumpet)
Released	2/26/1973 (US), 2/22/1973 (UK)
Chart Position	#1 (US Billboard 200) / #1 (UK Albums chart)
Sales	3x Platinum
Singles	"Daniel" "Crocodile Rock"

It's hard to imagine a rock album starting out more sedately than *Don't Shoot Me I'm Only the Piano Player*, which kicks off with, of all things, "Daniel"; but six albums in, Elton pretty much felt he could do whatever he wanted.

Don't Shoot Me was Elton's second straight album to go to #1 – and the first to generate a #1 single in the US - "Crocodile Rock". And "Daniel" came damn close to making it two, going as far as #2 (the songs his #5 and #4 in the UK, respectively. Elton had to fight like a madman to get "Daniel" released as a single at all[14], but its success made *Don't Shoot Me* the third straight album to produce two hit singles.

---

[14] See " Daniel", page 81.

Tracks

Side One
>**Daniel** (EJ/Taupin) - 3:54
>**Teacher I Need You** (EJ/Taupin) - 4:10
>**Elderberry Wine** (EJ/Taupin) - 3:34
>**Blues for Baby and Me** (EJ/Taupin) - 5:42￼
>**Midnight Creeper** (EJ/Taupin) - 3:55

Side Two
>**Have Mercy on the Criminal** (EJ/Taupin) - 5:57
>**I'm Gonna Be a Teenage Idol** (EJ/Taupin) - 3:55
>**Texan Love Song** (EJ/Taupin) - 3:33
>**Crocodile Rock** (EJ/Taupin) - 3:58
>**High Flying Bird** (EJ/Taupin) - 4:12

The Writing

As with "Daniel" and "Crocodile Rock", Bernie's themes for the rest the album were a pastiche. In "High Flying Bird", perhaps the album's best track, he analyzes a love gone wrong – a thread that would reach its apotheosis with "I Feel Like a Bullet (in the Gun of Robert Ford)" and "Sorry Seems to Be the Hardest Word" - while "Blues for Baby and Me" leans into psychedelia.

Bernie then picks up "Daniel"'s portraiture, serving up several poignant characters: "Elderberry Wine" is about a man who's lost his wife and is surveying his subsequent emptiness; "Midnight Creeper" is the tale of a moral low-life; "I'm Going to Be a Teenage Idol" is about a rock star wannabe, modeled on real-life glam rocker Marc Bolan.

The Music

Elton was in a borrowing mood in creating the music. Apart from raiding his youth for the innocent Happy Days riffs of "Crocodile Rock", author David Buckley notes that he looked to Derek and the Dominos for inspiration on "Have Mercy on the Criminal", and "Texas Love Song" lifts Fairport Convention's electric folk sound.

And that he even steals from himself on "Teacher I Need You",
recycling his rolling-triplet piano trick (that would become most
famous as the signature hook on "Pinball Wizard").

The Recording

For the second time, the band recorded at Château d'Hérouville, the
Honky Château, getting to work in June of 1972. But the album had
almost been pushed back to the fall.

"I made *Don't Shoot Me I'm Only the Piano Player* really on the edge of a
nervous breakdown," Elton said later. "I was so ill. I didn't know it, but
I had glandular fever and was very slow. When we first went over to
make it, *Honky Château* had just gone to #1 in the States and I said to
Gus, 'I can't make this album,' so he said, 'All right, we'll do it in
September.' Then I said, 'Wait, I'm going on holiday in July, it would be
nice to have it over by then.' It's a terrible way to look at it. So we did
it, although I was very ill and had some terrible rows. I don't think Dick
James and I spoke for four months after that."

Jacques Bolognesi (saxophone), Ivan Jullien (trumpet) and Jean-Louis
Chautemps (trombone), who had played on "Honky Cat" months
earlier, returned to play on "Elderberry Wine", "Midnight Creeper" and
"I'm Gonna Be a Teenage Idol".

Gus Dudgeon did the horn arrangements, while Paul Buckmaster did
the orchestrations.

Critical Response

Stephen Holden, *Rolling Stone: "Don't Shoot Me I'm Only the Piano
Player* is as good, if not better than its predecessor [*Honky Château*].
The heart of the album is a sequence of American movie fantasies
whose chief aim is to delight... Typical is the irresistibly catchy and
corny hit, 'Crocodile Rock.' More successfully than any recent single it
recaptures the spirit of late-Fifties rock 'n' roll, parodying styles ('At
the Hop' and 'Runaway') with such affectionate high spirits that the
song emerges as a genuinely fresh artifact of the Seventies. Elton's

tune and Taupin's lyric are ideally wedded. The song has a conventional verse-chorus structure and an overall diction that is casual and idiomatic without straining for precision: *"I remember when rock was young/Me and Susie had so much fun/Holding hands and skimming stones/Had an old gold Chevy and a place of my own."*

"The album's most moving cut, however, is the opener, 'Daniel.' A gem of technical virtuosity, it has Elton doubling on electric piano and 'flute' mellotron and Ken Scott on synthesizer, together making as deft use of the new electronic instrumentation as I've heard. Elton's melody and vocal are unusually tender and expressive, and Taupin's lyric, in which he recalls watching a plane carrying away his older brother, is exceptionally lovely..."

The album was Elton's first #1 in the UK.

It remained on the Billboard charts for 89 weeks.

What Elton Said

"The whole record's a total rip-off."

"It's got more balls [than *Honky Château*]."

"I really like some of the things on *Don't Shoot Me*... but as far as a continuous flow, it doesn't hold up. It's really a bubblegum album."

Factoids

Elton had mononucleosis when recording began.

The title came from an exchange between Elton and Groucho Marx, when Elton held up his hands and surrendered after a round of relentless ribbing from Groucho.

The album's release was delayed for six months to give a longer run on the charts.

Daniel

Written by	Elton John, Bernie Taupin
Chart position	#2 (US Billboard) / #4 (UK Singles Chart)
Released	3/26/1973
B-side	"Skyline Pigeon"
From the album	*Don't Shoot Me I'm Only the Piano Player*

"Daniel" was a surprise to radio listeners in the spring of 1973, following the likes of "Honky Cat" and "Crocodile Rock". It was an even bigger surprise for album buyers, who took home *Don't Shoot Me I'm Only the Piano Player* and heard the mild, contemplative "Daniel" right up front.

The Writing

Bernie's lyric was inspired by an article in a newsweekly concerning a Vietnam veteran who had been wounded in the Tet Offensive and wished to hide from the attention he was receiving upon returning. But Elton cut the verse that made that clear, making the meaning of the song obscure.

"The story was about a guy that went back to a small town in Texas, returning from the Vietnam War," Bernie said in the *Two Rooms* television special. "They'd lauded him when he came home and treated him like a hero. But he just wanted to go home, go back to the farm and try to get back to the life that he'd led before. I wanted to write something that was sympathetic to the people that came home."

Davey Johnstone explained the missing verse. "Elton had written this song which immediately we all loved. And he called me over and said 'Look at this last verse, I think Taupin's on drugs. He must be taking acid or something.' And we looked at this verse, and I can vaguely remember something about a ship's dog named Paul. And I'm like 'What the fuck is he talking about?' Suddenly out of nowhere he starts talking about this dog. So Elton just kind of took the page and ripped that bottom part off very slowly and very definitely and said 'Well, that's the end of that.' And that's why that verse was lost."

The Music

Rarely did Elton set aside the acoustic piano for the electric piano, but the song called for a gentle melancholy more suited to the latter. He described his music for the song as "a calypso-type number with Everly Brothers-type harmonies."

The Recording

The rest of the band took Elton's cue in supporting the song's tone. Davey played an easy-going acoustic rhythm guitar part; Nigel added unobtrusive maracas for rhythm. The signature flutey hook that opens the song was played (by Elton) on a Mellotron; engineer Ken Scott added ARP synthesizer in the solo.

"When I was in the middle of mixing 'Daniel', producer Gus Dudgeon decided Davey Johnstone's solo didn't 'pop,'" Scott said. "So I actually doubled the part on synthesizer."

The song was recorded on the day it was written, at the Château d'Hérouville in France – the "Honky Château".

The Response

Elton and Bernie were awarded the 1973 Igor Novello Award for Best Song Musically and Lyrically for "Daniel".

Among the misinterpretations of the lyrics were the suggestions that the song is about a family fight, a gay anthem, or a lost love.

What Elton/Bernie Said

Elton: "It is one of the best songs we've ever written. I don't care if it's a hit or not."

Bernie: "Regarding the missing verse that Elton cut – which has apparently been lost in time – Bernie said, "We had that whole thing about the missing verse that everybody seems to believe explained the true meaning of the song. I think that's just an urban legend. It didn't really explain anything. Sure, it was cut out. But that used to happen all the time with our songs. I would often overwrite, and Elton felt it necessary to edit somewhat. But believe me, it didn't say anything that the rest of the song didn't say."

Bernie on the character Daniel: "I don't have any set idea on who he is. I just started the song with that corny rhyme *plane* and *Spain*."

Cover versions

Wilson Phillips did a version on the album *Two Rooms*.

Lesley Gore covered it on her 1982 album *The Canvas Can Do Miracles*.

Fuel covered it on their album *Something like Human*.

Sam Smith did a version on *Revamp: Reimagining the Songs of Elton John & Bernie Taupin*, a tribute album released in 2018.

Factoids

Dick James didn't want to release the song as a single, feeling it wasn't lively enough (especially after "Crocodile Rock"), but Elton got pissy with him. He even insisted he would pay the promotional costs of the single if it tanked.

The younger of Elton's two sons is named Elijah Joseph Daniel Furnish-John.

Martin Scorsese used the song in his 1974 film *Alice Doesn't Live Here Anymore.*

Donatella Versace named her son after the song.

The running time is 3:54.

Crocodile Rock

Written by	Elton John, Bernie Taupin
Chart position	#1 (US Billboard Hot 100) / #5 (UK Singles Chart)
Released	11/20/1972 (US) / 11/27/1972 (UK)
B-side	"Elderberry Wine"
From the album	*Don't Shoot Me I'm Only the Piano Player*

Elton's first US #1 single was, on the one hand, a departure from the sound he and the band has carefully cultivated – and was, on the other, a perfect marriage of Bernie's thematic exploration and Elton's stylistic accommodation. "Crocodile Rock", conceived as a loving nostalgia fest, could scarcely have been more perfectly crafted.

The Writing

In addition to Elton's obvious homage to musical influences, Bernie slips one in with "…while the other kids were rockin' 'round the clock" - a tribute to Bill Haley and the Comets.

The song was the start of an extended review of his childhood, one that would continue into the songs of *Goodbye Yellow Brick Road*, as Bernie repeatedly revisited his teenage years.

The Music

Elton: "I wanted it to be a tribute to all those people I used to go and see as a kid. That's why I used the Del Shannon-type vocals and that bit from Pat Boone's 'Speedy Gonzales'. We also tried to get the worst organ sound possible."

Elton's list of cited inspirations is lengthy: In addition to 'Speedy Gonzales', it draws from Del Shannon's "Cry Myself to Sleep", "Let's Dance" by Chris Montez, "Little Darlin'" by the Diamonds, the Beach

Boys, Neil Sedaka's "Oh, Carol", Freddy Cannon, and the hit song "Eagle Rock" by Daddy Cool, among others.

The Recording

While backing vocals were normally done by Davey, Nigel, and Dee, on this song Elton did them himself. His intent was to preserve the gimmicky vocal style he was employing as part of his Fifties homage.

The Response

As Elton's first US #1 and first Gold single, "Crocodile Rock" was on top for three weeks. Although it didn't make #1 in the UK, it did stay on the charts for 14 weeks – the longest any Elton single had logged to that point.

In 1974, a lawsuit was filed in the US District Court of Los Angeles by Buddy Kaye, composer of Pat Boone's hit song "Speedy Gonzales", which Elton cited as inspiration, citing copyright infringement. The complaint specified that a chord sequence, as well as Elton's falsetto melody, were stolen from his song. Bernie and Elton settled.

Don McLean also complained that the song bore strong resemblance to his own Fifties nostalgia hit, "American Pie".

What Elton/Bernie Said

"I wanted it to be a record about all the things I grew up with," Elton said in response to accusations that the song was derivative. "Of course it's a rip-off, it's derivative in every sense of the word."

Bernie has said that while he thought the song was fun, it isn't one he'd go out of his way to hear.

Notable Covers

Cliff Richard covered the song in 1975 as part of a medley.

The Beach Boys contributed a version to the *Two Rooms* tribute album.

Alvin and the Chipmunks did a cover of it in 1990.

Factoids

Because the Farfisa organ sound is so integral to the song – and because Elton vamps like Jerry Lee Lewis when playing it live – sound engineer Clive Franks would leave the soundboard and go to the stage when it came time to play it, wearing one of Elton's silver lamé teddy boy jacket.

When guitarist Caleb Quaye joined Elton's touring band in 1975 as part of the shake-up that terminated Dee and Nigel, he did so on condition: that he not be required to play "Crocodile Rock".

The running time is 3:56.

Goodbye Yellow Brick Road

Produced by	Gus Dudgeon
Engineered by	David Hentschel
Performed by	Elton John (vocals, piano, electric piano, organ, mellotron) Davey Johnstone (acoustic/electric guitars, slide guitar, banjo, vocals) Dee Murray (bass, vocals) Nigel Olsson (drums, congas, tambourine, vocals Ray Cooper (tambourine) Leroy Gomez (saxophone) David Hentschel (ARP synthesizer) Kiki Dee (vocals) Del Newman (orchestration)
Released	10/5/1973
Chart Position	#1 (US Billboard 200) / #1 (UK Albums)
Sales	8x Platinum (US) / Platinum (UK)
Singles	"Saturday Night's Alright for Fighting" "Candle in the Wind" "Bennie and the Jets" "Goodbye Yellow Brick Road"

And now we come to Elton's masterpiece – *Goodbye Yellow Brick Road*, the greatest album in a deep shelf of great albums.

Many (including Elton himself) have called it his "White Album", and it's an apt comparison: like the Beatles' two-volume tome, it is packed with a variety of themes and characters, with no specific thread connecting them. It can be said of *GYBR*, however, that it presents consistency in its use of imagery, evoking the descriptor "cinematic" from many critics and observers.

"Cinematic" it certainly is, both overtly ("Candle in the Wind", "Roy Rogers", "I've Seen That Movie Too") and subtly ("Love Lies Bleeding", "Saturday Night's Alright for Fighting"). There are characters galore, from Bennie to Danny Bailey to Alice, a Sweet Painted Lady and a Dirty Little Girl.

"We were just more interested in creating very visual pieces of work that went beyond what people imagined the pop song of that time to be," Bernie said. "I don't know, maybe in retrospect it subconsciously is a concept album, because you're just presenting all these characters in this sort of cinematic framework. You're bringing up Danny Bailey and Sweet Painted Ladies and dirty little girls and, you know, they're all part of this big, sort of complex movie."

Said producer Gus Dudgeon of Bernie's extensive use of imagery: "Bernie loved the idea of setting up little pictures in your mind. It never mattered to him, necessarily, that the lyric told a story from front to back. What mattered to him was setting up a little cameo, little visual pictures in your mind, and if they didn't link together, well, so what? The important thing is, does it sound good when it's sung? Does it roll off the tongue well?"

"Each song had its own specific identity," said broadcaster Paul Gambaccini. "It wasn't just a love song, 'I miss you, I love you,' and then the next one is, 'I love you, I miss you'; you had 'Saturday Night's Alright for Fighting', 'Candle in the Wind', 'Bennie and the Jets' - I mean, completely different."

While some critics raved at the time of the album's release, others considered it a bloated, filler-heavy exercise in inexhaustible, self-indulgent music for masturbating junior-high boys. In the course of time, however, it has come to be regarded not only as Elton's pinnacle, but as one of the greatest albums ever made.

Tracks

Side One
    Funeral for a Friend/Love Lies Bleeding
        (EJ/Taupin) - 11:09
    Candle in the Wind (EJ/Taupin) - 3:50
    Bennie and the Jets (EJ/Taupin) - 5:23

Side Two

        Goodbye Yellow Brick Road (EJ/Taupin) - 3:13
        This Song Has No Title (EJ/Taupin) - 2:23
        Grey Seal (EJ/Taupin) - 4:00
        Jamaica Jerk-Off (EJ/Taupin) - 3:39
        I've Seen That Movie Too (EJ/Taupin) - 5:59

Side Three

        Sweet Painted Lady (EJ/Taupin) - 3:54
        The Ballad of Danny Bailey (1909-34) (EJ/Taupin) - 4:23
        Dirty Little Girl (EJ/Taupin) - 5:00
        All the Girls Love Alice (EJ/Taupin) - 5:09

Side Four

        Your Sister Can't Twist
                (But She Can Rock 'n Roll) (EJ/Taupin) - 2:42
        Saturday Night's Alright for Fighting (EJ/Taupin) - 4:57
        Roy Rogers (EJ/Taupin) - 4:07
        Social Disease (EJ/Taupin) - 3:42
        Harmony (EJ/Taupin) - 2:46

The Writing

Bernie: "A lot of my lyrics did come from the TV and movies I saw when I was younger. Like any other child of my generation in England, I grew up on American music, American movies and American television. All of my cinematic ideas were things like 'Roy Rogers,' 'Candle in The Wind' and 'Danny Bailey.' It's been said many times, but *Goodbye Yellow Brick Road* is a cinematic album. The lyrics to the title track do say that I want to leave Oz and get back to the farm. I think that's still my M.O. these days. I don't mind getting out there and doing what everybody else was doing, but I always had to have an escape hatch."

Bernie: "It's funny, but there are songs that I recall writing as if it was yesterday. And then there are those I have absolutely no recollection of, whatsoever. In fact, I'd have to say that for the most part, if someone was to say that the entire *Yellow Brick Road* album was actually written by someone else, I might be inclined to believe them. I remember being there, just not physically creating."

Bernie: "I have no memory of writing 'Love Lies Bleeding.' I have no idea where that came from. The same goes for 'Jamaica Jerk Off,' but I would imagine it was inspired by our adventure in Jamaica. A lot of the songs began when I came across a great first line. The perfect example is 'The Ballad of Danny Bailey.' I don't know if I'd seen a movie or read a book, but I came up with the first line, 'Some punk with a shotgun killed Danny Bailey/In cold blood in the lobby of a downtown motel.' And that was it. It would have gone a number of different ways, but it ended up being a tune about a bootlegger. Again, it was one of those cinematic stories."

The Music

Elton: "I didn't intentionally write the songs on that album in different styles. I grew up loving all sorts of music, and then I'm classically trained as well. That's where 'Funeral for a Friend' kind of comes in. And then 'Love Lies Bleeding,' the two of them weren't written together, we just stuck them together, and it worked. Things like that sometimes are a great surprise in the studio, little things just happen like that. Things like 'Sweet Painted Lady' is a very traditional kind of song. And then you have things like 'Bennie and the Jets,' which is completely off the wall."

The Recording

Production of the album initially began in Jamaica. The story is told in the 2001 *Classic Albums* documentary:

"We liked the idea of going away, and spending time together and writing together," said Elton. "The reason I chose Jamaica was because the Stones had done *Goat's Head Soup* there."

"So we basically packed up the caravans and rolled on out there," Bernie said, "and it basically just descended into shit, man! It was just a joke."

"The first sign we got that something might be a bit wrong was when the guy who ran the studio, we heard him say, 'Carlton! Get the microphone!'," Davey said, "and we're, Oh, fuck! 'Get the microphone?'

We used, like, twenty mics on the drums, even in those days! It's like, oh, we're in deep shit here..."

"And there was no gear in the studio," Nigel said. "And Gus is kind of looking around, 'Well, we need some 414s, and some 57s.' 'Don' worry, mon, it come tomorrow!' Well, tomorrow never came."

The problems with the setting went beyond the studio:

"There was barb wire around the studio, guys with machine guns, people yelling obscenities at us in the street. There wasn't one positive vibe in the place!" Bernie said.

"I don't know what happened," Elton said. "The studio workers were on strike, so we had to cross a picket line to get into the studio. That wasn't very pleasant. Then some of the equipment broke down. They kept saying they'd fix it tomorrow, but in the Caribbean, tomorrow can mean three days."

Bernie: "The climate was hospitable, but the natives weren't. To use the terminology of the time, it was not a 'good vibe.' I remember a lot of barbed wire around the studio and armed guards. We spent a lot of time congregating around the pool area of the hotel, feeling there was safety in numbers. The Stones did manage to record there, but in retrospect I think they had a mobile unit with them. The only thing I remember trying to record was 'Saturday Night's Alright for Fighting'. It was an aborted attempted, just atrocious."

"So we decided to leave early," Elton said, "and that didn't go down too well. They impounded our equipment, they took away our rental cars, and when Bernie and I were being driven to the airport, I thought, 'Omigod, they're just gonna kill us, they're gonna kill us!'"

"I remember everybody sort of jumping into whatever vehicles they could get in," Bernie said. "It was a bit like the sort of Cuban revolution, trying to make it to the airport. I imagine it was like the scene from *The Godfather Part II*, where everybody is just racing for the airport. It was our mini version of that!"

Escaping Jamaica, Elton and the band and studio team headed back to Château d'Hérouville, their Honky Château, where they'd previously recorded *Honky Château* and *Don't Shoot Me.*

"Actually, in retrospect, I think maybe it was preordained for that to happen," Bernie said, "simply because maybe we were so relieved to get out of there, it maybe gave us a new lease on life and a new enthusiasm for writing – because when we went to France, we wrote all of those songs in about two weeks."

"It wasn't technically the greatest studio in the world, but it was a great environment," said Elton. "It was funky, it had a good feeling."

That good feeling gave the band what it needed to bring *GYBR* to life. Everyone lived there together in the pastoral château, creating a communal atmosphere in which creativity was allowed to flourish of its own accord.

"Everybody seemed to be getting on very well," Bernie said. "Again, after the whole debacle of Jamaica, I think anything would have worked, we were so relieved. And it just became this very conducive kind of atmosphere to working. We'd write in the morning, and sort of just walk around the grounds, and go and record whenever we felt like it."

"I think, in those days, because we were a unit, because of my relationship with Bernie and the band and the management team and everything that went with it, it was just like a little family and it was great," Elton said.

"We were there, we were living together there as a family-type thing, for four weeks at a time," Nigel said. "We could see the songs being created, and it wasn't a case of Elton and Bernie sitting down together; Bernie had the lyrics, he gave them to Elton, Elton sat at the piano and started doing it."

"It was definitely right place, right time for us, that whole thing," said Davey. "It's was almost like we couldn't put a foot wrong. Everything we did was just the right thing; every part we put on was right."

The Two Rooms process, this time around, wasn't happening through the mail and in solitude; Bernie would bring his lyrics downstairs from his room and hand them to Elton, who would sit down at a piano and begin composing right there with the band.

"The way we'd write at the château would be, we'd have an area for breakfast where this little electric piano was set up and a little drum kit," Elton said. "So the band would learn it, and we'd learn it as I was writing it. And then we'd go over and record it."

"When the song was written, or rewritten, because of the Jamaica thing, we'd just go in and play it," Nigel said. "We were able to experiment, too. It was great. It was all whatever you felt."

Bernie's flood of images and Elton's stylistic oscillations didn't phase the others at all.

"The great advantage of having that band, and I must stress how important the band were to me, was that they knew, we all knew, different styles of playing, and everything gelled very quickly," Elton said. "As musicians, they just knew what to play on the songs."

The sessions were relaxed and intense at the same time: relaxed, because everyone was in harmonious frame of mind; intense, because they were producing music at a phenomenal rate.

"We probably did about four songs a day," Elton said. "Writing them, and recording them, plus overdubbing, plus vocals – it sounds insane, but that's the way it happened."

Elton: "On my first few albums, I didn't get to use my touring band. When I came to America in 1970, we'd been playing live for about a year or so in England and really doing the opposite to what the *Elton John* album was about. We played the same songs, but we played them in a completely rock n' roll style, piano, bass, and drums. When I did go to that momentous day at the Troubador in Los Angeles and I got the review from Robert Hilburn, it was a shock to people in the audience. They weren't expecting it, but that was how we were. I do think the band was a little wounded since they weren't on *The Tumbleweed Connection* or *Madman across the Water*. It was important to me that they play on *Goodbye Yellow Brick Road*."

This atmosphere also led to some of the greatest background vocals Elton's band ever produced ("Candle in the Wind" in particular).

"Davey, Dee and Nigel had this great blend together," Elton said, "and they'd say I should go away and I'd say Right, that's your job." ~Elton "Usually we'd do [backing vocals] at the very end of the album, after all the tracks were finished, all the lead vocals obviously were done," Davey explained. "Then Elton would bugger off, we'd get rid of him so we could really concentrate. If he's sitting around doing nothing, he's murder, complete murder, he's hell. So we'd get rid of him, and we'd concentrate on doing the backgrounds. And we used to really enjoy it because the combination of myself and Nigel Olsson and Dee Murray, who's unfortunately no longer with us, was really a special sound, just this blend, it was just brilliant. It was great fun to do and very inspirational to be a part of."

The sessions produced far more material than the band had ever managed on an album. The prospect of issuing a double album was raised.

"We always said we would never, ever do a double album," said Dudgeon, "because we could maybe think of what, three or four double albums that were worth bothering with? Most of them were just full of padding, most of them were rubbish. And we suddenly said, well, hang on a minute, if we actually were to throw out a couple of songs that aren't *that* great and look at what we've got left, maybe we *have* got a double album's worth of material."

"It wasn't hard, it wasn't an effort," Elton remembered. "It was a pleasure."

Critical Response

Goodbye Yellow Brick Road spent 1973 holiday season at #1 in the UK, holding that spot for two weeks – and sat four times as long at #1 in the US, from November into the new year. Certified gold in the States upon release, it had gone eight-times platinum by 2014, and since 2003 it has resided in the Grammy Hall Of Fame.

Rolling Stone's Stephen Davis: "This new record is a big fruity pie that simply doesn't bake. But, oh lord, how it tries. Elton plays in front of a thoroughly professional and creative instrumental group. Guitarist Davey Johnstone was a rare find when he joined the band a while ago: The guitar lines of the omnipresent AM hit 'Saturday Night's Alright for Fighting' ably testify to his power. Producer Dudgeon alternates tasteful and tricky ideas with lank orchestrations that owe more to Richard Perry and Mantovani than to music *per se*. By and large I can appreciate Bernie's lyrics, though the hatred of women that pervades this cycle of songs is *awesome* in its rancor — check the words to 'Dirty Little Girl,' that make the fabled Jagger-Richard demimonde sweethearts seem more like Karen Carpenter... What are we going to do with Elton John? He can sing, play, emote and lead a band, but he can't get organized. This would have made a lovely, if slightly brittle, single P. But the best tunes are obscured by drivel and peculiarly bad feelings. Not all fantasies are so rosy. Ugly ones mar a nice guy's record."

Typically, *Rolling Stone* changed its tune (2014): "The album was the biggest hit of their career, staying at #1 on the charts for two months and turning 'Bennie and the Jets,' 'Goodbye Yellow Brick Road' and 'Saturday Night's Alright for Fighting' into worldwide hits. There would almost certainly have been more had they released 'Candle in The Wind' and 'Harmony' as singles."

Chris Welch, *Melody Maker:* "superb new collection of songs... [Elton John and Bernie Taupin] surpassed themselves with a double-album that is bold, adventurous and vastly entertaining... a musical in its own right, ranging over a whole gamut of ideas and concepts...Beautifully produced by Gus Dudgeon, the sound of the Elton John band is occasionally blended with an orchestra, for special effects. But overall it is Elton's intense, frequently moving vocals, Davey Johnstone's guitar, Nigel Olsson's virulent drums, and above all the lyrics that create the greatest impression."

Lyricist Tim Rice: "I kind of think that the timing of the album was a very important factor. That's not to take away from its merit, but it came out at the moment when the world wanted Elton John, and he delivered, terrifically."

Paul Gambaccini: "For an artist to deliver a double album that crosses over to an extent that it's number one for eight weeks in America, sells six million copies – that's pretty fantastic."

Journalist Robert Sandall: "There aren't very many double albums made by really serious great artists. For some reason, when the acknowledged greats come out with double albums, it's usually because they are, in the modern parlance, 'on fire,' and they're worth it."

Sandall, continued: "I think, by the time he came to record *Yellow Brick Road*, he had really found himself as a musician and as a singer, and had discovered that his voice was one of the most versatile sort of rock voices that we'd heard, because he could sing flat-out slam-bam rock, and he could also sing ballads that were that were almost show tunes. And he could it without any sense of forcing it or parodying the stars involved. "

The album's trailing track, "Harmony", went on to win RKI's "Battle of the Hits", where listeners vote for their favorite track, 23 times in a row.

What Elton/Bernie/the Band Said

Elton: "I think it's a good collection of songs, brilliantly recorded by Gus Dudgeon, and brilliant played by me and the band."

Bernie: "I don't necessarily think it's our best album, but he was on fire, in the writing sense, and I guess I was, in the lyrical sense."

Elton: "*Electric Ladyland*, a couple of the Stones' albums, the Beatles' *White Album* – I'm not saying it's as good as them, but I think, quality-wise, it ranks up there."

Bernie: "I just guess it hits a note with people, the people who sort of grew up with us, that's maybe the strongest point – it's the sort of karmic root to everything that we've done since then or before that."

Bernie: "I don't know if we set out to make a double album. I think it was just the quality of the songs and the amount of them that we had in the end…I think it was the pinnacle of our career at that point."

Elton: "We could have put out other singles like 'Harmony' and sold even more records. In those days, a record was off the radio after eight or nine weeks. These days, you look at the Adult Contemporary charts and it's like, 'Are you fucking kidding me? This record came out two and a half years ago!' We could have kept going with singles, but we'd already finished *Caribou* by the time 'Bennie and the Jets' came out as a single. We were ready to move on."

Davey: "We were playing stuff off of *Yellow Brick Road* [live] before the album was out. This was just part of the tour. We were giving those fans a little taste of something they'd never heard. It never occurred to us not to do it."

Elton John: "I didn't even know what a joint was when I made *Goodbye Yellow Brick Road*. That all changed when I made the next record, but in 1973 I was very naïve. And the naiveté is the most pleasant thing about this record, probably."

Bernie Taupin: "That's very true. Drugs didn't really come into play until right afterwards when we made *Caribou* and *Rock of the Westies*. The only thing I ever remember him doing was smoking a little dope back in the late 1960s in the studio with Dick James. But that's about it."

Elton: "It was a very exciting time in my life. It was a time that we had no fear, nothing was beyond us. It's a wonderful thing the young have when they get on a roll. We were running on momentum and adrenaline. And then if you're a talented enough artist, you find your place within the playing field. And this was our example of being at the height of our creative powers."

"It was magic. That time in my life, that creative period, will never, won't ever come back again. You search for it, and you try and think, oh, it'd be great to do, but it'll never happen like that again."

Factoids

In 2014, a 40th anniversary deluxe edition of *Goodbye Yellow Brick Road* was issued, including nine cover versions of songs from the original album by artists such as Ed Sheeran, Fall Out Boy, and the Zac Brown Band. The five-disc set also includes a 1973 live show from the Hammersmith Odeon and a DVD documentary, also from 1973.

The album's working titles were *Vodka and Tonics* and *Silent Movies*.

Bernie wrote all the lyrics in two and a half weeks.

The album is #91 on *Rolling Stone*'s all-time 500 Greatest Albums of All Time.

The album's iconic cover painting is the work of Ian Beck.

Funeral for a Friend

The instrumental that opens Side One of the magnificent *Goodbye Yellow Brick Road*, by far the most perfect album side of Elton's career, had a complex origin.

The song began with Elton, not Bernie; as it is lyric-free, that makes sense. His starting point was imagining what music he would want played at his own funeral.

"Funeral" opens with the sound of whistling wind and a distant bell-tone, moving through a dirge of minor-key synthesizer chords, executed by ARP synth expert David Hentschel[15], who was also *Yellow Brick Road*'s primary engineer.

It proceeds into a more pronounced dirge – Elton at his piano – unveiling a-B theme to Hentschel's A-theme – marching through a complex series of key changes, rising and rising with much anxiety as Davey joins the fray with a frenetic takeover of the melody as synth lines snake into Elton's chords, funeral-marching to a stiff halt, as Elton starts hammering his piano in an A-minor rage.

The C-theme blasts apart its solemn predecessor with smashing chords lashed to an angry melodic line. Two passes, and Nigel and Dee join in, and the theme roars forward, culminating in a teeth-gnashing, synth-soaked crescendo, then crashing down into the middle of the B-theme, with Davey catching the ball, through a series of chord changes, leading Elton into the D-theme, a melodramatic chromatic walk-up that gives Dee space for some lightning bass runs, until the whole thing drops out to Just Elton again, with the synth whispering in above him.

Elton is in the home stretch, and starts chording what will become "Love Lies Bleeding"; Davey helps him forward with some staccato punches, and almost six minutes in, "Funeral" shakes off its sweat...

"Funeral" is wedded to the song "Love Lies Bleeding" - one track segues into the next. The composite track runs 11:08. But this was not

---

[15] Ever the economist, Hentschel raided *GYBR* tracks "Danny Bailey", "Candle in the Wind", and "I've Seen That Movie Too" for melodic fragments.

by design; they were two separate tracks. Producer Gus Dudgeon had the idea of splicing them together (by coincidence, "Funeral" ends in the key of A, and "Love Lies Bleeding" begins there) - and once he had done so, he showed it to Elton and convinced him the two songs should become one long track. Elton came up with some transitional material to close the seam.

Donald Guarisco of *AllMusic* called the result "A stunning instrumental, [with] a powerful fusion of classical and rock elements where a gentle, lyrical motif is developed and energized until it builds into a powerhouse full of emotion and bombast."

Billboard rated it #2 in the list of Elton's best songs picked by critics ("Bennie and the Jets" topped it); *Rolling Stone*'s readership rates it #3 among Elton's "Deep Cuts".

The song is most famously covered by the progressive rock unit Dream Theater, who included it on their 1995 album *A Change of Seasons*. The progressive band Redemption likewise covered it on their 2011 album *This Mortal Coil*.

Elton and his band opened their 2001 album *One Night Only* with Side One of *Goodbye Yellow Brick Road*, thus performing "Funeral/Love Lies Bleeding" in its blistering entirety.

Saturday Night's Alright for Fighting

Written by	Elton John, Bernie Taupin
Chart position	#12 (US Billboard Hot 100) / #7 (UK Singles Chart)
Released	7/16/1973
B-side	"Jack Rabbit" / "Whenever You're Ready (We'll Go Steady Again)"
From the album	*Goodbye Yellow Brick Road*

The first single from *Goodbye Yellow Brick Road* was, by far, the hardest-rocking thing Elton had ever put out. Based on Bernie's memories of his raucous teenage years, it was simultaneously menacing and endearing, with the celebration of youth shining out over images of shattered beer mugs and broken bar stools.

The song continues its parent album's parade of cinematic images, and is simultaneously a throwback to an earlier rock era. Elton's performance on the piano recalls Jerry Lee Lewis, and the song overall smells like the Rolling Stones.

It has remained a constant presence in Elton's shows for 40+ years. It is one of the top 10 most performed tracks in his canon, having been performed live more than 1,300 times.

The Writing

"I'd started to feel I was writing too much about American culture and American things," Bernie said. "'Saturday Night' was my first attempt to write a rock-n-roll song that was totally English."

"So much of my imagery at that time came from my childhood," Bernie said. "I mean, 'Saturday Night's Alright for Fighting' totally recalls when I was like, fourteen, fifteen, going to all these places in the north of England... it was just too much beer and Bang! Somebody would start a fight and it was all over the place."

"It was steeped in the days of mods and the rockers and all the sort of confrontations," according to Bernie. "It was just a straightforward 'Saturday night's alright for drinking, fighting, getting screwed up'..."

The Music

"A lot of the power of that song comes from the chords," Bernie said. "I mean, it has one of the great, strident, blistering guitar chords ever created. You don't even have to wait for the lyrics to come it."

The Recording

"Saturday Night" was the only song from Goodbye Yellow Brick Road to be recorded in Jamaica, before the band and recording team abandoned that effort and transplanted the album to the Honky Château. It was, however, re-recorded once they'd relocated: "When we played [the Jamaica version] back in the studio, it sounded like it had been recorded on the worst transistor radio ever."

Playing and singing with the band, Elton just couldn't get it the song down.

"Right," he told the band, "You three just play the fucker and I'll sing it and we'll do the piano later."

The Response

"The perfected 'Saturday Night's Alright for Fighting' preceded the album as a summer 1973 single," wrote Paul Sexton of udiscovermusic.com in 2019. "Its pugnacious, high-testosterone feel matched a lyric based on Taupin's true experiences, from his days of under-age drinking at the Aston Arms, in the Lincolnshire town where his secondary school was situated, Market Rasen."

What Elton/Bernie Said

Elton: "I vividly remember recording "Saturday Night's Alright for Fighting.' I couldn't seem to get the piano part right, so when the band played bass, drums and guitar, I laid on the floor did the vocal live. And then I put on my piano part afterwards. It's an odd way of doing it. But I remember doing that because it felt, for some reason, the four of us, me playing live, it just didn't work. So I overdubbed my piano afterwards and sang the vocal live."

Bernie: "Over the years you tend to invent your own myths about songs because you feel it's necessary to come up with a reason why you wrote a certain song. It's been said on so many occasions that 'Saturday Night's Alright for Fighting' relates to my English past. People says, 'Oh, Bernie wrote it about a pub he used to hang out and get into fights at.' It's quite possible there's a germ of truth in that. Did I say to myself, 'I'm going to sit down and write a song about my childhood watching the mods fight the rockers?' No, I don't think that I did. With so many of my songs, the lyrical content has been misconstrued, misinterpreted and you get to the point where you feel like you have to make something up in order to make somebody happy."

Notable Covers

The list of covers of "Saturday Night's Alright for Fighting" is not only long, but distinguished:

The Who covered it on *Two Rooms* in 1991.

Queen covered it on their unofficial Italian release of the same name in 1991.

Nickelback included it on their 2003 album *The Long Road.*

The heavy metal outfit W.A.S.P. released it as a CD single in 2000.

It also made an appearance in the movie *Kingsman: The Golden Circle*, which starred Taron Egerton, who played Elton in *Rocketman*. It was also featured in the movie *Grand Theft Auto*.

Factoids

Side Two's contents, "Jack Rabbit" and "Whenever You're Ready (We'll Go Steady Again)" were leftovers from the *Don't Shoot Me I'm Only the Piano Player* sessions.

The running time is 4:12.

Goodbye Yellow Brick Road

Written by	Elton John, Bernie Taupin
Chart position	#2 (US Billboard) / #6 (UK Singles Chart)
Released	10/15/1973
B-side	"Screw You" ("Young Man's Blues")
From the album	*Goodbye Yellow Brick Road*

Countless fans and critics consider "Goodbye Yellow Brick Road" to be Elton's best song ever. It is melancholy and majestic; it is orchestral in scope, yet coffeehouse-intimate. It is his most daring vocal ever, atop emotionally evocative chord progressions that are symphonic in their affect.

And it is a departure, lyrically, from any terrain Elton and Bernie had yet explored. The lyric is deeply personal, and yet it seems to have a range of meanings.

While not the most successful song of Elton's career – that would be "Candle in the Wind 1997" - it may be the one rock history embraces the longest... and it isn't even a rock song.

The Writing

The Yellow Brick Road itself obviously came from *The Wizard of Oz* – the first movie that both Bernie and Elton had ever seen. The rest of the song was about his self-reflective inner quest to recover himself after years strapped to Elton during his meteoric journey.

"Bernie's reflective lyric is an early and telling indication that fame was becoming all too much for the lad from Lincolnshire," wrote rock historian David Buckley. "'I should have stayed on the farm, should have listened to my old man'. It's a song about disillusionment, and was the first by Bernie to reveal a road-weariness and a desire for something postfame, 'beyond the Yellow Brick Road.' The Emerald City of fame and fortune was evidently bringing as many hardships as benefits. Bernie wanted out – 'I'm going back to my plough.' There would be many, even darker-themed sons from Bernie as the 1970s unfolded."

"There was a period when I was going through that whole 'got to get back to my roots' thing, which spawned a lot of like-minded songs in the early days, this being one of them," he said. "I don't believe I was ever turning my back on success or saying I didn't want it. I just don't believe I was ever that naïve. I think I was just hoping that maybe there was a happy medium way to exist successfully in a more tranquil setting. My only naiveté, I guess, was believing I could do it so early on. I had to travel a long road and visit the school of hard knocks before I could come even close to achieving that goal. So, thank God I can say quite categorically that I am home."

"The song is also a thinly-veiled reference to Judy Garland," wrote rock historian Elizabeth Rosenthal. "Intriguingly, an album by an artist who had not yet gone public about his sexuality contained songs about two icons of the gay community: Marilyn Monroe and Judy Garland."

The *"mongrels who ain't got a penny, sniffing for tidbits like you"* was inspired by Linda Woodrow's two dogs.

The Music

Elizabeth Rosenthal describes the music as follows: "This [melody] is strikingly visual," she wrote in *His Song: The Musical Journey of Elton John*. "Like some graceful winged creature, it glides over the scene of the malcontent who retreats to the yellow brick road, finally swooping downward as descending chords portray his grudging steps homeward. This melody, so ably interpreted by all the band's instruments, the orchestration, and the singular backing vocals, makes for an unexampled musical sojourn."

Elton came up with the chord progression that opens the song before anything else.

The Recording

Recorded, like almost all the songs from the *GYBR* album, at the Honky Château, "Goodbye Yellow Brick Road" was set to tape on the day it was written, in that communal setting where band and engineering crew all lived and worked together day in and day out in the pastoral fields north of Paris.

"The vocal, it sounds like it's sped-up. I don't know why he did that, he just went out there and sang it in this sort of sped-up voice," said producer Gus Dudgeon. "And a lot of people thought, a lot of people asked me if I'd sped the tape up, but in fact it's not sped up; it's just the weird way he decided to do it. That's Elton."

The Response

Rolling Stone's Stephen Davis, in his review of the *GYBR* album: "The title tune that starts side two is real wimpy too, dedicated to some poor showbiz shlubbo who the boys say they're not going to have anything to do with in the future."

Much later, *Rolling Stone* changed its tune (as it so often does). In *Rolling Stone*'s *100 Greatest Singers of All Time*, Ben Folds described Elton's vocal: "He was mixing his falsetto and his chest voice to really fantastic effect in the Seventies. There's that point in 'Goodbye Yellow Brick Road' where he sings, *'on the grooound'* - his voice is all over the shop. It's like jumping off a diving board when he did that."

It's No. 380 on *Rolling Stone*'s list of The 500 Greatest Songs of All Time.

"I think the strength of 'Yellow Brick Road', or certainly something that contributes to its lasting appeal, is the fact that it does actually reflect on the dark side of life, and to some degree the dark side of celebrity, which at that time Elton John was just starting to feel." ~Journalist Robert Sandall

"I think when you have success, your first reaction is 'Yippee!' And your second reaction, in the words of Peggy Lee (or Jerry Leiber), 'Is that all there is?' I think, probably, if we think about it, that was about the time when Elton and Bernie had realized that they'd made it. They were two or three years down the road, and they were very successful. And I guess, on reflection now, you can see, even if Bernie didn't mean it at the time, there is a bit of 'I'm not sure it's what I want.' Often the fulfillment of an ambition can be worse than not fulfilling it." ~Tim Rice

What Elton Said

"Maybe he was getting disillusioned," Elton said of Bernie's lyric, "but I certainly wasn't. I was having a ball!"

Notable Covers

Billy Joel, in his 1994 box set *A Voyage on the River of Dreams* (A live version featuring Elton and Joel performing the song as a duet in Madison Square Garden can be found on *One Night Only*).

Queens of the Stone Age covered it on the 2018 tribute album *Revamp: Reimagining the Songs of Elton John & Bernie Taupin*:

"It's nice to pick something that may seem off kilter at first for us to do. But 'Goodbye Yellow Brick Road' really has the psychedelic carousel nature to it," said Josh Homme of Queens of the Stone Age. "I think at first we thought we will tinker with the arrangement, but there's so many beautiful chords - the chord progression is so wonderful - once you step on that carousel, it's just this beautiful musical swirl and it's really intoxicating to be on that carousel. And it seemed like there's a psychedelic element that we could bring out, that it's touching on, and that maybe the key for us to do it would be to accentuate the wispiness that is going on in the song."

Ray Conniff, on his 1974 album *The Way We Were.*

Factoids

At the time of its release as a single, "Goodbye Yellow Brick Road" set a record for chart life – 16 weeks. That record stood until 1983, when Elton's "I Guess That's Why They Call It the Blues" topped it.

Ben & Jerry's created an Elton-themed flavor of ice cream: *Goodbye Yellow Brickle Road*. Introduced in 2008, on the occasion of Elton's first show in Ben and Jerry's native Vermont, it included chocolate ice cream, peanut butter cookie dough, chunks of white chocolate and butter brickle.

At the famous Dodger Stadium concerts, Elton replaced the words "It'll take you a couple of vodka and tonics" with "It'll take you a couple tequila sunrises."

The single's B-side, "Screw You", had to be retitled "Young Man's Blues" for release in the US, at MCA's insistence.

The running time is 3:11.

Candle in the Wind

Written by	Elton John, Bernie Taupin
Chart position	#6 (US Billboard Hot 100) / #11 (UK Singles Chart, 1974) / #5 (UK Singles Chart, 1988)
Released	2/4/1974
B-side	"Bennie and the Jets"
From the albums	*Goodbye Yellow Brick Road /* *Live in Australia with the Melbourne Symphony Orchestra*

The most successful song in Elton's catalog, "Candle in the Wind" was a hit not once but three times: it was the second single from Goodbye Yellow Brick Road in England (it wasn't released in the US at that time); it was a hit again in 1988 in a live incarnation from Elton's Australia concert album; and it became the biggest hit single of all time in 1997, when Elton and Bernie rewrote it as a tribute to Princess Diana[16].

For all that, neither Elton nor Bernie can even remember writing it.

The Writing

"You know what? I don't remember writing it. And I don't remember him playing it to me," Bernie said. "I really don't. What I do remember is, I remember the title. But I don't remember writing it, or hearing it for the first time."

Bernie: "I always loved the phrase. Solzhenitsyn wrote a book called 'Candle in the Wind', and Clive Davis, I remember, used it as a term to describe Janis Joplin. And I just, for some reason, kept hearing this term. I thought, what a great, great way of describing somebody's life."

Bernie: "I wrote 'Candle in The Wind' about Marilyn Monroe, but she is absolutely not someone I admired a lot as a kid or anything. She was just a metaphor for fame and dying young, and people sort of

[16] See "England's Rose", page 197.

overdoing the indulgence, and those that do die young. The song could have easily have been about Montgomery Clift or James Dean or even Jim Morrison. But it seemed that she just had a more sympathetic bent to her, so I used her. And she was female, and that was more vulnerable. But it was really about the excesses of celebrity, the early demise of celebrities, and 'live fast, die young, and leave a beautiful corpse.' And that was really the crux of the song."
Bernie: "I wanted to say that it wasn't just a sex thing. That she was someone everybody could fall in love with, without her being out of reach."

The Music

"For me, it's a beautiful song – but I can't really remember writing it."
~Elton

The Response

Rolling Stone: "'Candle in the Wind' is the first heavy lyrical fantasy, the tune is prettily solemn and unbelievably corny, a necrophiliac erection for Marilyn Monroe, despite the disclaimer: 'Goodbye Norma Jean/From the young man in the 22nd row/Who sees you as something more than sexual/More than just our Marilyn Monroe.' Oh, bullshit."

Tim Rice: "It's not just the fact that it's about Marilyn Monroe... it's about all people who were misjudged in their lives; it's a song about unfairness and the destruction of reputation. And I think a lot of people, even if they haven't been through that themselves, they can understand it in their heroes."

What Elton/Bernie Said

Bernie: "To be quite honest, I was not *that* enamored with Marylin Monroe. What I was enamored with was the idea of fame, or youth, or somebody being cut short in the prime of their life. I mean, basically the song could have been about James Dean, it could have been about

Montgomery Clift, it could have been about Jim Morrison, anyone whose life is cut short at the prime point of their career, and how we glamorize death, how we immortalize people. And that's really what that song is about."

Elton: "I was a huge Marilyn Monroe fan, as well as Elvis Presley. When you saw them, they looked like they came from another planet. In the Fifties when I had my hair cut and I first saw a picture of Elvis Presley in *Life* magazine, I thought, 'My God, who is this guy?' And with Marilyn Monroe, it's like, 'That's the most glamorous woman that's ever been.' I mean, her and Elizabeth Taylor…There will never be two more glamorous people. And they kind of changed the world."

Bernie: "I'm sure there are people out there that would be happy if they never heard 'Candle in The Wind' again. But the thing is, if a song gets into the lexicon that way, that means it's probably a good song. I think it's one of the best marriages of lyric and melody that Elton and I have ever put together. But it doesn't change the fact that I wasn't particularly enamored by Marilyn Monroe."

Bernie: "Nobody's allowed to die an honorable or quiet death. I mean, we cannot leave it alone; we have to always find something to keep it alive. And all those elements are encompassed in that song."

Notable Covers

Billy Joel performed the song during the 1994 *Face to Face* concert.

Wham! covered the song in their 1986 farewell concert (Elton played piano).

Kate Bush did a version for the flip side of her 1991 single cover of "Rocket Man".

Ed Sheeran contributed a version to the 40th anniversary edition of *Goodbye Yellow Brick Road*. He covered it again in 2018 on the tribute album *Revamp: Reimagining the Songs of Elton John & Bernie Taupin*.

The English punk band Leatherface covered it on their 1990 album *Fill Your Boots*.

Sandy Denny, an English folk artist, did a version on her 1977 album *Rendezvous*.

The Shadows did an instrumental version on their 1989 album *Steppin' to the Shadows*.

Factoids

The song had never been released as a single in the US, but got a second chance when Elton included it in his live concert in Australia in December 1986. The resulting album, Live in Australia with the Melbourne Symphony Orchestra, yielded the US single that had been missing the first time around – a single that went to #6 on the Billboard Hot 100.

The song also topped its previous release in the UK, this time ascending to #5.

While the album version is lush, with soaring, atmospheric vocals, the live version is sparse: just Elton at his piano, with subtle backing keyboards by Fred Mandel.

On April 7, 1990, Elton performed the song at Farm Aid IV, dedicating it his AIDS-stricken young friend Ryan White. Ryan died the next day.

The original track is #347 on *Rolling Stone*'s list of The 500 Greatest Songs of All Time.

The running time is 3:50.

Bennie and the Jets

Written by	Elton John, Bernie Taupin
Chart position	#1 (US Billboard Hot 100) / #1 (UK Singles Chart) / #15 (US Billboard Hot Soul Singles)
Released	2/4/1974
B-side	"Candle in the Wind" / "Harmony"
From the album	*Goodbye Yellow Brick Road*

Elton's not-rock, not-pop story of a fictional glam rocker and her band was in fact Bernie's send-up of the 1970s music industry, poking fun at its greed and excesses. It is simultaneously a wide-eyed embrace of fandom, which both Elton and Bernie had not only faithfully respected but only recently emerged from themselves.

"To this day, I can't see 'Bennie and the Jets' being a hit," Elton told *Classic Albums* in 2001, "and I fought tooth-and-nail against it coming out from the *Yellow Brick Road* album." He was fearful that the single would fail, and that would be the end of his momentum.

Not only did the song go to #1 in both the US and UK – it went Top 20 on the US Hot R&B chart.

The Writing

Bernie: "I saw Bennie and the Jets as a sort of proto-sci-fi punk band, fronted by an androgynous woman, who looks like something out of a Helmut Newton photograph."

The Music

Elton: "When I saw the lyrics for 'Bennie and the Jets,' I knew it had to be an off-the-wall type song, an R&B-ish kind of sound or a funky sound. The audience sounds were taken from a show we did at the Royal Festival Hall years earlier. The whole thing is very weird."

The Recording

The song's great fame derives largely from its novelty, not only as a wild stylistic carom off the rest of Elton's canon, but for its contrived pose as a live track. Producer Gus Dudgeon took the tracks, recorded with the rest of *Goodbye Yellow Brick Road* at the Honky Château, and doctored them at the mixing console to sound live.

"We put on some sounds effects which were basically from an Elton concert at a festival that he'd done about four or five years before," said Dudgeon. "You've got Jimi Hendrix's applause from the *Isle of Wight* [album] which was running on a loop, which we just faded in whenever we wanted to; we threw a load of flapback on it to make it sound live; dubbed on some whistles and handclaps doing the wrong beat, because English audiences *always* do the wrong beat, they're always on the on instead of on the off, which drives me crazy, but that's what they do."

The Response

Heavy airplay on CKLW in Windsor, Canada pushed the song to #1 in Detroit, and from there it went viral on US and Canadian Top 40 stations. It went gold eight weeks after its release.

Rolling Stone's Stephen Davis: "I like the end of the side, "Bennie and the Jets," a wimpy *Sgt. Pepperish* number (even to the point of dubbed audience noise) about a mythical rock & roll band. Elton's vocal is properly dramatic and funny too."

As a result of the song's R&B chart success, Elton and the band were invited to appear on *Soul Train* in May 1975. They played "Bennie" and "Philadelphia Freedom".

"It was getting a lot of play on black radio at the time," Bernie recalled. "There was a guy at Universal Records called Pat Pipolo - for some reason I always remember his name, probably because he was the one who was so gung-ho about releasing it."

"[Elton] said, 'Are you willing to put your career on the line over something like that?,'" Pipolo recalled. "I said well, no, not really, but I think we should release it as a single. I think you'll be an R&B artist as well as a pop artist. So he called the main office and he told them what we should do with 'Bennie and the Jets', and we did, we released it, and sure enough, it went to Number One Pop, as well as Number One R&B. Which amazed the world, I think, and certainly amazed Elton."

"He was accepted at all the black stations, which was amazing," said Rick Frio of MCA. "I mean, Elton John, English kid? It didn't happen. I think the only other person from England maybe was Dusty Springfield. Yeah, it was unusual."

What Elton/Bernie Said

"It's the strangest track on the whole album," Elton told *Circus* magazine. "It's a send-up of the glitter rock thing, and I sound like Frankie Valli of The Four Seasons."

"Never in a million years, being a white boy from Pinner, did I ever think I was gonna have a black record on the charts." ~Elton

Notable covers

Elton has performed the song with Cher and Christina Aguilera.

The Beastie Boys covered it on their 1999 album *The Sounds of Science.*

Pink and Logic covered the song on the 2018 tribute album *Revamp: Reimagining the Songs of Elton John and Bernie Taupin.*

The organist for the New York Knicks, Ray Castoldi, plays the song at Knicks home games.

Factoids

The song was famously called out in the 1992 comedy movie *Wayne's World* for its popular mis-heard lyric, "She's got electric boobs, a mohair suit..." There are a number of variations, including "She's got electric boobs, and mole hair, too..." And it's not the only one: many listeners get to the line "We'll fill the fatted calf tonight, so stick around" and hear "A killer fight in the parking lot, so stick around."

Axl Rose said that when he was a teenager, "Bennie and the Jets" meant a lot to him.

The title was incorrectly spelled "Benny" on the sleeve of the single.

The running time is 5:23.

Caribou

Produced by	Gus Dudgeon
Engineered by	Clive Franks, David Hentschel
Performed by	Elton John (vocals, piano, Hammond organ) Davey Johnstone (acoustic/electric guitars, mandolin, vocals) Dee Murray (bass, vocals) Nigel Olsson (drums, vocals Ray Cooper (tambourine, congas, whistle, vibraphone, snare, castanets, tubular bells, maracas) Lenny Pickett (saxophone, clarinet) David Hentschel (ARP synthesizer, mellotron) Tower of Power (horns) Chester Thompson (Hammond organ) Bruce Johnston, Carl Wilson, Toni Tennille, Clydie King, Sherlie Matthews, Jessie Mae Smith, Dusty Springfield, Billy Hinsche (backing vocals)
Released	6/28/1974
Chart Position	#1 (US Billboard 200) / #1 (UK Albums)
Sales	2x Platinum (US)
Singles	"Don't Let the Sun Go Down on Me" "The Bitch is Back"

The Honky Château had been a haven for the band since the album named for it, remaining so through *Don't Shoot Me*, and *Yellow Brick Road*. It was time for a change.

That change was a new recording venue, for which the album was named: Caribou Ranch, a studio located in the Colorado Rockies near Nederland, built by producer James William Guercio[17] in 1972. The

---

[17] Guercio is himself a rock legend, though not a household name: he played guitar in Frank Zappa's Mothers of Invention, produced Blood Sweat & Tears, and created the band Chicago. He managed the Beach Boys in the 1970s and toured with them as a member of their band. He won the Album of the Year Grammy for the second BS&T album.

studio was built in an old barn on a ranch. It was surrounded by cabins, where visiting musicians and studio personnel would stay while recording.

Davey: "*Caribou* was an extraordinary experience because the château had become a comfort zone. We'd done three (sic) albums there. Then it was like, 'Well, we've heard about this place, Caribou Ranch.' I was very familiar with *Barnstorm*, Joe Walsh's album that was done there. I was like, 'Oh, shit. Yeah, let's go there. That sounds perfect.' We went there in the dead of winter, early January. That'd become a ritual. We'd start the year off with a new album regardless of the fact that we'd done a couple in the middle of the year also. We went there January in 1974, I believe.

"There was like 10 feet of snow. We all had our own log cabins. We were told, 'Wear this parka or you'll freeze to death on the way to the studio. Wear snow boots. We've got snowmobiles. You guys can go up and try, have fun on these during the day.' When I went out there to the snowmobile area, who should be tuning up the snowmobiles other than Terry Kath of Chicago? He basically took his parka off and I'm going, 'Shit, you're Terry Kath,' and we struck up a big friendship."

Elton and the band would continue recording at Caribou through *Rock of the Westies*.

Tracks

Side One
> **The Bitch is Back** (EJ/Taupin) - 3:44
> **Pinky** (EJ/Taupin) - 3:54
> **Grimsby** (EJ/Taupin) - 3:47
> **Dixie Lily** (EJ/Taupin) - 2:54
> **Solar Prestige a Gammon** (EJ/Taupin) - 2:52
> **You're So Static** (EJ/Taupin) - 4:52

Side Two
>   **I've Seen the Saucers** (EJ/Taupin) - 4:48
>   **Stinker** (EJ/Taupin) - 5:20
>   **Don't Let the Sun Go Down on Me** (EJ/Taupin) - 5:36
>   **Ticking** (EJ/Taupin) - 7:33

The Writing

After the astounding run of *Tumbleweed*, *Madman*, *Honky Château*, *Don't Shoot Me* and *Yellow Brick Road*, it could be that Bernie was simply burnt out.

Caribou certainly had good moments; the two singles, "The Bitch is Back" and "Don't Let the Sun Go Down on Me", are both stand-outs in the Elton canon. But with the exception of "Ticking", the final track – the disturbing story of a troubled young man who goes on a killing spree in Queens – the songs have almost no substance.

"Solar Prestige a Gammon", for example, is literally gibberish – *Kool kar kyrie kay salmon, Har ring molassis abounding.* The speculation is that the song was written to intentionally push back against the now-ubiquitous search for meaning in Elton's song by critics and cultural observers.

The Music

If Bernie was phoning it in, Elton did better. Though not as inspired as his Honky Château work had been, *Caribou* contains some really good stuff.

On "Stinker", for instance, he went for a traditional blues number with some rock energy; for "Mellow", a song about intimacy, he created music that felt as gentle and romantic as Bernie's lyric. "You're So Static" turned out badly, but Elton's flamenco piano made for an interesting experiment. On the album's token country-esque track, "Dixie Lily", a song about a riverboat, he breaks out the honky tonk he'd spent two years perfecting.

Not his finest hour, but by and large his contribution to Caribou was stronger than everyone else's.

The Recording

"*Caribou* is a piece of crap," according to Gus. "The sound is the worst, the songs are nowhere, the sleeve came out wrong, the lyrics weren't that good, the singing wasn't all there, the playing wasn't great, the production is just plain lousy."

Perhaps so, but there are some splendid moments. "Ticking", for instance, had its dark content offset by sparse, uncomplicated accompaniment: the only instruments used were Elton's piano and David Hentschel's synthesizer. More interesting still, Elton played and sang simultaneously, which is very unconventional procedure in studio recording, despite the track's length – he was concerned that if he tried to play the piano track alone, he'd have to think too hard about it.

Davey's blistering guitar intro on "The Bitch is Back" owes much to Pete Townsend's blistering guitar intro on the original "Pinball Wizard". It makes sense that this was in Davey's mind, as Elton and the band recorded their cover of the Who tune for the upcoming *Tommy* film at the same time.

"I've Seen the Saucers", an inexplicable song about UFOs, drew great percussion out of Ray Cooper, who managed to animate the song with congas and a gong.

Beach Boys Carl Wilson and Bruce Johnston appear on *Caribou* because the Beach Boys were trying to record there at the time.

Critical Response

Tom Nolan, *Rolling Stone*: "What John and Taupin have excelled at is the assembling of commercial sounds. Their recorded creations have been carefully constructed pop artifacts, the end product of controlled experiments in which element is added to element, a process more akin to making objects than to making music. Whatever's trendy is sure to catch their attention and find its way into their mix. They take pride in being on top of things, in writing the first astronaut single, in fashioning the definitive nostalgia hook, in marketing the timely eulogy to Marilyn. Elton John makes records in the same manner as he puts together his wardrobe and choreographs his concerts. Often what he mistakes for style is simply next month's bad taste, but discrimination does not really concern him. It needn't matter if something's grotesque; what's important is that it's new. Elton is an impresario of stance, a maestro who has presented a series of attractive aural surfaces. The trouble with surface is that it wears thin.

"*Caribou* is not wearying in the same way as would be an album whose makers were bored with their work. *Caribou* is dispiriting because it *logically* extends Elton's weak strengths and strong weaknesses, the superficial powers that have taken him so far. The thin roots that kept him in touch with an organically nourishing topsoil have been sundered and at last he's on his own, fulfilling his weird hybrid nature in a self-designed hothouse where nothing but lurid display is valued.

"Nearly every song on *Caribou* suffers from a blithe lack of focus, an almost arrogant disregard of the need to establish context or purpose. It's as if Elton and his band are so convinced of their own inherent inspiration they no longer feel the need to establish coherent moods. Shifting from sentimental to heavy to mocking, they not only fail to touch all bases but undercut what credence they might possibly have achieved."

What Elton Said

Elton, to *Melody Maker*: "It was recorded under the most excruciating of circumstances. We had eight days to do 14 numbers. We did the backing tracks in two and a half days. It drove us crazy because there was a huge Japanese tour, then Australia and New Zealand, that could not be put off. It was the first time we recorded in America, and we couldn't get adjusted to the monitoring system, which was very flat. I never thought we'd get an album out of it."

Factoids

Many artists recorded at Caribou Ranch, including Earth, Wind & Fire, Supertramp, Carole King, Dan Fogelberg, Billy Joel, Rod Stewart, Badfinger, Waylon Jennings and Amy Grant. Chicago recorded five albums there. The studio burned down in 1985.

Caribou received a Grammy nominated for Album of the Year in 1975.

Don't Let the Sun Go Down on Me

Written by	Elton John, Bernie Taupin
Chart position	#2 (US Billboard Hot 100, 1974) / #16 (UK Singles Chart, 1974) / #1 (US Billboard Hot 100, 1991) / #1 (UK Singles Chart, 1991)
Released	5/20/1974, 11/25/1991
B-sides	"Sick City" (1974) / "I Believe (When I Fall in Love It Will Be Forever) (1991)"
From the albums	*Caribou / Love Songs / Greatest Hits 1970-2002 / Duets*

"Don't Let the Sun Go Down on Me" may be Elton's most bombastic single ever. It is certainly one of the grandest, with its huge, choir-like choruses and magnificent horns. What makes the song stand out in the canon is the song's dynamic range; for all the pomp of the choruses, the verses are very stark – just Elton and his piano, with subtle touches of guitar and percussion surfacing phrase by phrase.

Bernie's lyrics and Elton's vocal take the song past every previous one they'd done in a similar vein; the song is about distance between two people who loved each other, coping with rejection and disappointment. Elton is at his most vulnerable, and the power of the choruses convey the sheer magnitude of the alienation and grief expressed in the lyric.

It's no surprise that, like "Candle in the Wind", the song kept coming back again and again in Elton's story.

The Writing

The idea behind the song, Bernie said, was to write a love song that was naked in its pain.

"I like to be more interesting than a good old 'I love you, you love me, my heart will break if you leave me," he said in an interview with *Esquire*. "Throw in a curveball. 'Don't Let the Sun Go Down on Me.' Put a dark twist on them."

The goal was to write a really *big* song, he said: "My only recollections of this is that we wanted to write something big. I mean, big in that dramatic Spectory [Phil Spector] style, like 'You've Lost That Lovin' Feelin'". Hopefully being powerful without being pompous. I'm not sure that with this in mind it made me fashion the lyrics any differently. Although, in retrospect, they do seem to have a slightly more Brill Building flair to them, so it's entirely possible that I did."

The Music

In writing the music, Elton said he was influenced by the Beach Boys – their "sound, harmonies, and the way they structured their songs" - and in fact two Beach Boys, Bruce Johnston and Carl Wilson, sang on the song.

The Recording

There are two stand-out aspects to the recording of "Don't Let the Sun Go Down on Me". The first is the astounding backing vocals, which were a Who's Who in Pop/Rock fest; the second is Elton's bitch rant.

Going big on the vocals meant bringing in some heavyweights. Heavyweights they were indeed: in addition to two Beach Boys, Dudgeon brought in The Captain and Tennille – Toni Tennille and Daryl Dragon, who were red-hot in pop music at the time - as well as Dusty Springfield (who had sung backing vocals on the earliest Elton albums), as well as some members of America and Three Dog Night.

Bruce Johnston and Daryl Dragon wrote the arrangement for the backing vocals, and Gus recorded all those voices. In the end, however, he only kept the parts sung by the Beach Boys and Toni Tennille; the entire ensemble sounded terrible. (Billy Hinsche is also credited with backing vocals.) Oddly, Davey, Dee, and Nigel, whose backing vocals had become so powerful over the last few albums, weren't used at all.

As for Elton's demeanor in the session, Gus Dudgeon said, "When Elton recorded this track, he was in a filthy mood. On some takes, he'd scream it, on others he'd mumble it, or he'd just stand there, staring at the control room. Eventually, he flung off the cans and said, 'Okay, let's hear what we got.' When I played it to him, he said, 'That's a load of fucking crap. You can send it to Engelbert Humperdinck, and if he doesn't like it, you can give it to Lulu as a demo.'"

Nigel: "He got so frustrated that he couldn't get this one line [that] he screamed at Gus Dudgeon, 'Screw this! Send it to Lulu, and if she doesn't like it, send it to Engelbert!' But five minutes later it was fine."

The horns, arranged by Del Newman, were done by Tower of Power, who appeared on the tracks of many artists, notably Huey Lewis and the News.

Engineer David Hentschel, who played ARP synthesizer on a number of previous tracks, added mellotron. Ray Cooper, by this time a member of Elton's touring band, provided tambourine and bells.

"Don't Discord Me"

One of the famous quirks of the song is Elton's pronunciation of the word "discard" in the final version – he says "discord", for no clear reason.

"There was one bit on Elton's vocal I really wanted to bury," Gus said. "When he sang the line "Don't discard me", he put on this really ridiculous American accent, so it came out "Don't discord me". But Toni Tennille said, 'No, leave it. It sounds good.'" Smart move; that odd line became part of the song's unique character.

The Response

Alongside "The Bitch is Back", the other single from the album, "Don't Let the Sun" launched *Caribou* into the stratosphere on both sides of the Atlantic, sending it to #1. The song was Elton's fourth Gold single.

It peaked at #2 in the US, kept from ultimate glory by John Denver's "Annie's Song" and Paper Lace's "The Night Chicago Died".

"[It] is arguably the greatest one Elton and Bernie have ever written," said rock journalist Elizabeth Rosenthal. "Though there have been better marriages of lyric and melody among Elton's and Bernie's traditional ballads – the tightly-written 'Candle in the Wind' and, later, 'Nikita' - "Don't Let the Sun" carries on the grand tradition of the Elton John panoramic ballad. Here, he takes the genre steps further with music that sweeps the listener effortlessly along, from the hurtful despair of the opener to the brave, declarative, hopeful chorus. The song's bare parts, purely heard during the verses, delicately brush the listener. Nigel's cymbal compliments Elton's opening piano notes, which plead in heartsick descent. Within seconds, the individual notes join for the rumble of prefatory descending chords, and Elton delivers a sweet, lonely vocal of pure misery to match his melody of unbridled sadness. Backed by some chirping acoustic and electric guitar strokes by Davey, Elton sings to someone he has helped and from whom he is now experiencing rejection. The chorus swells into one of the most recognizable anthems, becoming a symphony supported by Del Newman's horn arrangement and the notable backing vocals of the Beach Boys' Carl Wilson and Bruce Johnston, and Toni Tennille. The voices combine with well-timed percussion accents from Ray Cooper and surreptitious mellotron from Dave Hentschel for a collective musical catharsis, a virtual emptying of the soul."

"The video was actually shot over several days," said George Michael's publicist Michael Pagnotta of the famous Elton surprise concert footage George Michael released in 1991. "It was shot in an airplane hangar in Burbank, California where George had been rehearsing; Elton came in for a night and they ran through the song a couple of times. Then the song was filmed in its entirety live in Chicago in the middle of October as part of that Cover to Cover tour, and when Elton came out from the wings, that place went crazy."

The 1991 George Michael duet version of the song was nominated for a Grammy Award for Best Pop Vocal Performance by a Duo or Group.

What Elton Said

"This is my Beach Boys tribute," Elton told journalist Robert Hilburn. "I was always so much influenced by them, especially Brian Wilson."

Elton has said in interviews that he would never have tried to sing a song like "Don't Let the Sun Go Down on Me" earlier in his career, believing that his voice wouldn't have been up to it.

Notable Covers

Roger Daltry of The Who covered the song in 1987. His version was included in the film *The Lost Boys*.

Joe Cocker covered it on his 1991 album *Night Calls.*

Oleta Adams covered the song on the *Two Rooms* tribute album. Her version was released as a single, notching #33 in the UK.

Factoids

Elton included the song in his *Live in Australia* concert and released an edited version of it as a single in 1987.

Proceeds from the 1991 single were divided between 10 different charities.

Guns N' Roses drummer Matt Sorum has said that "Don't Let the Sun"'s drum track influenced his own performance on three GnR tracks, after Axl Rose played him the song to show him Nigel's use of tom toms. The songs were "November Rain", "Don't Cry" and "Estranged".

British pop flash-in-the-pan Nik Kershaw, a formidable singer-songwriter in his own right, scored his first hit single with his song "I Won't Let the Sun Go Down on Me", which bears no resemblance whatsoever to Elton's tune. Kershaw has said that Elton is an inspiration, and that "Your Song" was the first record he ever bought.

The running time is 5:47.

The Bitch is Back

Written by	Elton John, Bernie Taupin
Chart position	#4 (US Billboard Hot 100) / #15 (UK Singles Chart)
Released	9/3/1974
B-sides	"Cold Highway"
From the album	*Caribou*

Once again, Elton made the radio with something utterly different than anything he'd ever done before. "The Bitch is Back" was not just risqué; it was unabashed, self-deprecating, autobiographical, and roared like nothing he'd put on radio before, excepting "Saturday Night's Alright". The song became a joyous self-parody, with Elton mocking his own lifestyle.

Some radio stations refused to play it at first; but demand for the song was so great that they relented in the end, adding it to their playlists[18].

The Writing

Bernie got the idea from his wife Maxine, who went with the band on tour and got accustomed to Elton's tantrums and stompy fits. When Elton would begin a rant, she'd turn to Bernie and say, "The bitch is back!"[19]. Bernie wrote it up, and Elton in his best good-sport manner embraced the song, making it his anthem.

The Music

Elton's goal, in creating a song immortalizing his immaturity, was to make the track as flamboyant and over-the-top as himself. He gave the song the same exuberance found in "Crocodile Rock", but paced it for

---

[18] Some stations applied coping mechanisms: a few restricted the song from drive time but played it in the evenings; some put the song in rotation, but the disc jockeys would not announce the name of the song.

[19] See "Blue Jean Baby", page 49.

Davey, rather than himself, realizing that it needed to be a wide-open guitar rocker.

The Recording

Sticking with his overall approach to Caribou, Gus brought in extra backing vocalists (including Dusty Springfield). He also used the Tower of Power horns, as he had on "Don't Let the Sun Go Down on Me".

Lenny Pickett was used for the saxophone solo in the middle of the song.

The Response

In New York, WPIX-FM's program director told Billboard magazine, "We will play records that are borderline suggestive records such as 'Disco Lady'... but we will not play 'The Bitch is Back' by Elton John. We won't play those types of records no matter how popular they get."

Elton responded, "Some radio stations in America are more puritanical than others."

Tom Nolan, *Rolling Stone*: "'The Bitch Is Back' is the slickest and strongest cut on *Caribou*, but it lacks real punch. The combined forces of Clydie & Sherlie & Jessie & Dusty and the Tower of Power horn section fail to get this putdown-celebration of a certain sort of social pariah-piranha off the ground."

What Elton Said

Elton: "It is kind of my theme song."

Notable Covers

Tina Turner did the song for years in her live show. Her version is notable for her refusal to sing "I get high in the evening sniffing pots of glue," singing instead, "I get high from the speaking 'bout the things I do." Her version appears on her 1978 album *Rough*, her 1988 *Live in Europe* album, and the *Two Rooms* tribute album.

Lita Ford included it on her albums *Living Like a Runaway* and *The Bitch is Back...Live.*

The heavy metal band Bitch covered it on their 1987 album *The Bitch is Back*.

Billy Joel has performed the song in concert, with and without Elton.

Miley Cyrus did a cover of it for the 2018 tribute album *Restoration: Reimagining the Songs of Elton John & Bernie Taupin.*

Factoids

In 1974, the word "bitch" had never been heard in a radio hit. Among those stations that refused to play the song, a few tried to edit it out. But the word occurs 42 times in the song, so those edits sounded absurd.

In the November 1974 Madison Square Garden show that featured a surprise appearance by John Lennon, Lennon played tambourine on "Bitch"[20].

At one of Elton's triumphant Dodger Stadium shows, Billie Jean King[21] got up on stage with Elton and danced to "Bitch".

[20] Gus Dudgeon added this live recording to the re-issue of *Here and There.*

The Rolling Stones had included a song titled "Bitch" on 1971's *Sticky Fingers*, but didn't release it as a single.

Two decades later, the word "bitch" had gone mainstream, so no one blinked when Meredith Brooks released her single "Bitch", which was an immediate feminist hit.

"Bitch" is the only song of Elton's that rock critic Dave Marsh thought good enough to be included in his book *The Heart of Rock and Soul: The 1001 Greatest Singles Ever Made.*

The song was used by the conservative group Free Republic to demean Hillary Clinton during her 2003 book tour, showing up and playing the song loudly. Clinton was amused.

The video used behind the song in Elton's *Red Piano* show in Las Vegas features Pamela Anderson pole-dancing.

The running time is 3:42.

---

[21] See " Philadelphia Freedom", page 132.

Music and Lyrics by Ann Orson/ Carte Blanche

Elton John and Bernie Taupin were famous for their "Two Rooms" approach to songwriting, with Taupin generating a pile of scribbled lyrics which he would hand off to Elton, who would sit down and pound out music for each one. The two were never in the same room at the same time, writing songs.

But this formula, while hugely successful, wasn't absolute: from time to time Elton would do some lyric scribbling of his own.

This actually began before he was Elton John – as Reg Dwight of Bluesology, he wrote a tune called "Come Back Baby" all by himself. Shortly after becoming Elton, he wrote "Here's to the Next Time", the B-side of his first-ever single, "I've Been Loving You", in 1968.

A decade later, EJ wrote "Flintstone Boy", B-side of the single "Ego", with no Taupin assist.

Occasionally he co-wrote with Bernie, as when he tacked a third verse onto "Border Song" - changing the theme of the song in the process. And sometimes he acted as Bernie's editor, as when he ripped a verse out of "Daniel" (a verse in which it was made explicit that brother Daniel was a Vietnam veteran). He did the same in the less-familiar "Holiday Inn" (from *Madman Across the Water*).

Finally, there were times when Bernie edited Elton: the latter's first pass at lyrics for a Kiki Dee duet - "Don't Go Breaking My Heart", which went to No. 1, the first UK chart-topper for them both – fell into Bernie's hands, and he "cleaned them up". This teamwork was given its own moniker: the song is credited to "Ann Orson/Carte Blanche", a pseudonym for the two of them.

And that trick was repeated yet again, when Elton wrote Kiki a track - "Hard Luck Story" - as a single just for her, but then re-recorded it for "Rock of the Westies".

Philadelphia Freedom

Written by	Elton John, Bernie Taupin
Chart position	#1 (US Billboard Hot 100) / #12 (UK Singles Chart)
Released	2/24/1975
B-side	"I Saw Her Standing There"
From the album	*Elton John's Greatest Hits, Volume II*

The Writing

Elton had met tennis icon Billie Jean King in 1973, and a friendship immediately sprung up between them. Elton approached Bernie about writing a song for her, suggesting "Philadelphia Freedom" as an homage to King's tennis team, the Philadelphia Freedoms.

Both the name and the city evoke patriotism, and the song became a pseudo-patriotic anthem, especially in America's following bicentennial year.

What Bernie produced, however, had nothing to do with either tennis or patriotism. King herself had said she didn't want the song to actually be about tennis, saying that "Philadelphia Freedom" "...is a feeling." Bernie has since claimed that the lyrics mean nothing.

The song was conspicuously planned as a single, not an album track – the first such single in their partnership.

The Music

The song is dedicated to "the Philadelphia sound," which to EJ meant soul music.

After doing a rough-mix demo of the song at the Caribou Ranch, Elton presented the song to King. "He was so nervous that I wasn't gonna like it," she said, "but I loved it. It's just so thoughtful that they wrote a song and dedicated it to me. It meant a lot."

The Recording

The song was recorded at Caribou during the summer of 1974, during breaks in the *Captain Fantastic* sessions. It was a stylistic departure for the band: Dee plucked the bass part to make it punchier, and Davey played slide guitar.

The orchestration, which included strings, horns and woodwinds, was done by Gene Page, who had orchestrated tunes for Barry White. Side Two of the single contained the live recording of the Beatles' "I Saw Her Standing There", Elton's duet with John Lennon at Madison Square Garden the previous November.

The Response

Though the song went to #1 in the US, it stalled at #12 in the UK. This may owe in part to a conflict between Elton and the British TV show *Top of the Pops*, which was crucial to the success of any new single by a British artist. The conflict arose because of a rule in place with the British Musicians Union stating that any song performed on television had to have a specially-recorded orchestral track. Elton's position was that British session men were not competent to reproduce Gene Page's parts accurately, and offered his own recording. *Top of the Pops* declined, so Elton refused to appear, to the detriment of the single.

Billie Jean King went on to partner with Elton in a number of charitable endeavors, including fundraising for HIV/AIDS research.

What Elton/Bernie Said

Bernie: "I can't write a song about tennis."

Elton: "In America I've got 'Philadelphia Freedom' going up the charts again. I wish the bloody thing would piss off. I can see why people get sick and tired of me. In America I get sick and tired of hearing myself on AM radio. It's embarrassing."

Notable covers

Hall & Oates did a version for the 1991 *Two Rooms* tribute album.

MFSB did a cover of it in 1975 and named the album on which it appears after it.

Factoids

When Billie Jean King played Bobby Riggs in the famous "Battle of the Sexes" tennis match in 1973, Elton was watching on television in a hotel room, and cheered so hard for her that he lost his voice.

Percussion Ray Cooper is featured in the photo on the sleeve of the single as a full member of the band.

The single is credited to "The Elton John Band", rather than to Elton himself (this was also true of the previous single, "Lucy in the Sky with Diamonds", though the photo on the sleeve of that single was of Elton alone).

When Elton was invited to play "Bennie and the Jets" on *Soul Train*, he also played "Philadelphia Freedom".

The lyrics of "Philadelphia Freedom" are printed on the wall at Philadelphia's Hard Rock Café.

Billboard ranked "Philadelphia Freedom" as #3 among songs of 1975.

The running time is 5:20.

Captain Fantastic
and the Brown Dirty Cowboy

Produced by	Gus Dudgeon
Engineered by	Jeff Geurcio
Performed by	Elton John (vocals, piano, electric piano, clavinet, mellotron, ARP synthesizer, harpsichord) Davey Johnstone (acoustic/electric guitars, mandolin, piano, vocals) Dee Murray (bass, vocals) Nigel Olsson (drums, vocals Ray Cooper (tambourine, congas, shaker, jawbone, gong, bells, cymbals, triangle, bongos) David Hentschel (ARP synthesizer) Gene Page (orchestration)
Released	5/19/1975
Chart Position	#1 (US Billboard 200) / #2 (UK Albums)
Sales	3x Platinum (US)
Singles	"Someone Saved My Life Tonight"

After the horrific misfire of *Caribou*, Elton and Bernie needed a reboot. Bernie suggested a strong one: write about what they knew best – themselves.

Captain Fantastic and the Brown Dirt Cowboy is the story of their friendship/ partnership, a reliving of their pre-fame adventures. The album is a masterwork, on a par with *Yellow Brick Road* (if not as accessible). It is, in many ways, stronger than its predecessor, a unified narrative that Bernie actually wrote in chronological order.

Gus Dudgeon, who had been so disparaging of *Caribou*, had nothing but praise for *Captain Fantastic*: "It's the best that they've ever played, it's the best that he's ever played, and it's the best collection of songs. There's not one song on it that's less than incredible."

It would be the last album that the classic band would record together until *Too Low for Zero* in 1983.

Tracks

Side One

> **Captain Fantastic and the Brown Dirt Cowboy**
> (EJ/Taupin) - 5:46
> **Tower of Babel** (EJ/Taupin) - 4:26
> **Bitter Fingers** (EJ/Taupin) - 4:35
> **Tell Me When the Whistle Blows** (EJ/Taupin) - 4:20
> **Someone Saved My Life Tonight** (EJ/Taupin) - 6:45

Side Two

> **(Gotta Get A) Meal Ticket** (EJ/Taupin) - 4:01
> **Better Off Dead** (EJ/Taupin) - 2:37
> **Writing** (EJ/Taupin) - 3:40
> **We All Fall in Love Sometimes** (EJ/Taupin) - 4:15
> **Curtains** (EJ/Taupin) - 6:15

The Writing

In Bernie's autobiographical document, Elton is the Captain and he is the Cowboy.

"Captain Fantastic and the Brown Dirt Cowboy" establishes the two characters, portrayed as wide-eyed boys whose sense of wonder is quickly blunted by the realities of growing up poor. The lyric begins with a presentation of innocence, progressing through disappointment into resolve.

"Tower of Babel" is a derisive attack on Dick James, as the heroes doggedly pursue their songwriting dream and collide with the ugly truths of the publishing industry.

"Bitter Fingers" chronicles the compromise of writing songs to order, for other artists – something they were forced to do before Elton took the stage.

"Tell Me When the Whistle Blows" returns to Bernie's love of the country, restating his longing to return home.

"Someone Saved My Life Tonight" combines Elton's goofy suicide attempt[22], failed engagement to Linda Woodrow, and his rescue by Long John Baldry.

"(Gotta Get A) Meal Ticket" is a starving-artists story, detailing the songwriters' struggles to get by in their early days.

"Better Off Dead" sits somewhere between the despair the two felt at the time and their role as observers of the world around them, taking in the struggles of the people they would see on the streets.

"Writing" takes a positive turn, reflecting on the days when Elton and Bernie were writing songs specifically for their budding stage career, and the growing bond between them.

"We All Fall in Love Sometimes" is a song about a song, chronicling the composition of "Your Song", and expresses their feelings for one another.

"Curtains" ends the story, summarizing all that has changed for them during their journey thus far. It references "Scarecrow", Elton's first-ever demo.

The Music

Because the songs were about himself, rather than just another batch of Bernie myths, Elton felt more personally connected to them, and that manifested itself as a deep investment in the music he composed.

"That album was about the two of us, the things we'd been through together and what it all meant thus far," Elton said. "It felt so good to be writing songs that I not only understood the lyrics to but was a complete part of. Before, I was singing stuff that perhaps didn't directly relate to me."

---

[22] See "The Worst Suicide Attempt Ever", page 57.

The Recording

While all the previous albums had been produced in days, *Captain Fantastic* took almost a month, so careful were Gus and the band in crafting it. Sitting in the engineer's chair next to Gus was Jeff Guercio, younger brother of studio owner James, replacing David Hentschel.

That time was used very effectively. Given a sheaf of lyrics that were, for once, more story than image, Gus worked with Elton's music to create musical imagery.

In the title cut, for instance, the West is evoked by Davey's acoustic guitar and mandolin; in "Tower of Babel", the Biblical references are given an operatic push by newcomer Ray Cooper's punchy percussion; Davey's guitar is like a divine finger etching lines under Elton's piano melodies. The desperation of "(Gotta Get A) Meal Ticket" is perfectly expressed by Davey's blaring guitar; the dream-like etherea of "Someone Saved My Life Tonight" is introduced through Elton's soft electric piano chords and synthesizer pads.

Critical Response

Captain Fantastic shipped Gold and was #1 the week it was released – the first album in history to do so.

Jon Landau, in *Rolling Stone*: "This is one of Elton John's best albums. He hasn't tried to top past work, only to continue the good work he's been doing. And he's succeeded, even taking a few chances in the process... There's no illusion of saying something, they *are* saying something; there's no illusion of a superb performance but a superb performance itself; no imitation of quality but rock of very high caliber."

Broadcaster Paul Gambaccini: "*Captain Fantastic* is a serious album; it's not for laughs. Not for nothing was the booklet for *Goodbye Yellow Brick Road* accompanied by illustrations, because Bernie had a way of conjuring up the visual. You can see it as well as hear it. *Captain Fantastic* wasn't image-driven, it was autobiographical, so it's almost as if part of the dimension of Elton John was not there. As a strictly musical achievement it is at least it's equal, but it doesn't have the pop culture plusses that *Goodbye Yellow Brick Road* has."

It is #158 on *Rolling Stone*'s list, The 500 Greatest Albums of All Time.

What Elton/Bernie Said

Elton: "Before I just used to write melodies to Bernie's experiences and fantasies. I identify with this album so much more than anything else I've done. For me it will always be my favourite album. But that's from a purely selfish point of view. Whether it will stand the test of time, who knows? You can only tell in retrospect."

Elton, in an interview with Cameron Crowe: "I've always thought that *Captain Fantastic* was probably my finest album because it wasn't commercial in any way. We did have songs such as 'Someone Saved My Life Tonight,' which is one of the best songs that Bernie and I have ever written together, but whether a song like that could be a single these days, since it's [more than] six minutes long, is questionable. *Captain Fantastic* was written from start to finish in running order, as a kind of story about coming to terms with failure - or trying desperately not to be one. We lived that story."

Bernie: "For me, *Captain Fantastic* will always remain an entirely satisfying work, possibly the only album we have ever made where every track fit into a cohesive pattern free of any corrupting elements. It's time in a bottle, a potent capsulated snapshot of a crucial period in our lives that helps to remind me that nothing comes easy."

Factoids

Elton and the band played the album in its entirety in concert at Wembley Stadium in the summer of 1975. The show was horrible, according to Davey Johnstone, but a live recording of it was included in the 2005 30th Anniversary Deluxe Edition of *Captain Fantastic*.

However, when they did so again at Madison Square Garden in 2005, the show went wonderfully.

Elton's 2006 album *The Captain and the Kid* is a sequel to *Captain Fantastic*, picking up the autobiographical story where it left off.

The Worst Suicide Attempt Ever

Among the drama queens of rock, Elton John certainly looms large – stories of his rants, tantrums and melodrama are legend.

Still, even the most ridiculous melodrama can morph into magnificent music – and Elton, along with songwriting partner Bernie Taupin, were well-equipped for such transformations.

The magnificent music is Elton's "Someone Saved My Life Tonight", from his concept album *Captain Fantastic and the Brown Dirt Cowboy* – his 12th Top 10 single, which peaked at #4. One of his moodiest works, this somber ballad is more than a little cryptic and dark, yet in the end oddly inspiring, even so.

Its origins are, put simply, just goofy.

Not yet realizing he was gay, the 21-year-old Elton John became engaged to the first girl he slept with, one Linda Woodrow, and the two found themselves living in Bernie's flat in Highbury. Elton became increasingly anxious over the impending nuptials, falling into such a state that he decided to end it all.

He decided gas was the way to go, and turned on the oven – but to ease the discomfort of his passing, he found a comfy pillow to lay his head on.

And left the kitchen windows open.

So hilarious was this attempt that Taupin was a long time letting him forget it – and, of course, the incident found its way into his songwriting notebook.

Long John Baldry took Elton aside and reasoned with him that the thing to do was abandon the idea of marriage and focus on his career. Seven years later, when Taupin penned the song, Baldry was immortalized as "Sugar Bear" - he is the 'someone' referenced in the song's title.

The story of the song has a great postscript. During the recording of *Captain Fantastic*, Elton was having trouble nailing the lead vocal. His longtime producer Gus Dudgeon grew impatient, pushing him harder and harder to really let loose with it.

Guitarist Davey Johnstone, in the control room with Dudgeon, leaned quietly in and said, "You realize he's singing about killing himself..." Mortified, Dudgeon backed off and let Elton finish the track[23].

Trivia tidbit: at 6:45, the song is Elton's longest single.

---

[23] This story is told by Paul Gambaccini in the liner notes of the Deluxe Edition of *Captain Fantastic*.

Someone Saved My Life Tonight

Written by	Elton John, Bernie Taupin
Chart position	#4 (US Billboard Hot 100) / #22 (UK Singles Chart)
Released	6/23/1975
B-side	"House of Cards"
From the album	*Captain Fantastic and the Brown Dirt Cowboy*

Like everything else on *Captain Fantastic*, "Someone Saved My Life Tonight" is autobiographical, emerging from the shared journey of Elton and Bernie. Specifically, the song is about Elton's comical 1968 suicide attempt[24], and his not-so-comical engagement to Linda Woodrow.

The Writing

Bernie: "It tells a story that actually happened. For the most part, most of the things I write are an amalgam of several subjects or feelings that I then cut and paste to create one entity. Not always, but a lot of the time, I mean, I guess you could even say that with this song, the crux of its meaning is sort of surrounded with visual props that are intended to help set the scene for the main event, which was Elton saying *adios* to this woman who was pushing him into a marriage that he knew deep down in his heart would be a lie on a multitude of levels."

Bernie: "It's packed with imagery, like most of the songs from [*Captain Fantastic*]. I was most definitely trying to conjure up an atmosphere and project a moment in time when we were struggling with the mundane areas of life, the everyday struggles to make ends meet. So when I hear that song now, it really makes me think of grey skies and wet streets, smoky pubs; in all, that fragile feeling you just kind of get inside when you're unsure of the future."

---

[24] See "The Worst Suicide Attempt Ever", page 57.

Elton: "I was going to get married once when I was younger, and I went out and got drunk with Long John Baldry and Bernie and John said I shouldn't get married. I knew he was right, but I didn't know how to get out of it, so I just got drunk and went home and said I'm not getting married."

The mystery line "...paying your H.P. demands forever" refers to a Hire Purchase Packet, which is a kind of installment loan where payments are deducted from one's paycheck. The use of the line suggests that the singer is paying for his lover's luxurious purchases.

"They're coming in the morning with a truck to take me home" sounds like men in white coats are on the way, but this is a literal reference to Elton's stepfather Derf showing up the morning after Elton broke off the engagement with a van at the basement flat where Elton and Bernie were living with Linda to gather up their things.

The Music

Elton was aboard the *SS France* on a cruise when he wrote the music. Because there was an opera singer on board who booked most of the piano time, he had to wait for opportunities to use it and write in short bursts.

It was the final voyage of the *SS France*.

Part of his inspiration for the music came from Brian Wilson: "I thought about Brian Wilson and 'God Only Knows'," he said. "From the first chord you can tell that."

The Recording

The classic band plus percussionist Ray Cooper (adding tambourine, shaker and cymbal) were all Gus used to lay down the track. Elton himself played the ARP synthesizer, which was used on the song's later choruses.

During the recording, Gus browbeat Elton into improving a vocal performance that was hesitant and lackluster, not realizing the emotional content of the song. "I made him sing the most unbelievably personal things over and over again to get a bloody note right or get a bit of phrasing together!" Realizing what the confrontation was doing to Elton, out in the studio, Davey set Gus straight.

The Response

Jon Landau, *Rolling Stone*: "As long as Elton John can bring forth one performance per album on the order of 'Someone Saved My Life Tonight', the chance remains that he will become something more than the great entertainer he already is and go on to make a lasting contribution to rock."

"Seldom had a pop song been so poetic, so perfect, and yet so blistering in its attack on one person's psychological and emotional dominance over the other. This was a very public retaliation." ~Rock journalist David Buckley

Because it was so personal, Elton refused to cut the song down for airplay. It went to #4 in the US anyway, despite being almost a minute longer than "Bohemian Rhapsody".

Elton's use of the word *"dammit"* in the second verse caused some radio stations in the US to ban the song.

Following the song's release, Linda Woodrow said in interviews that she harbors no ill will for Elton and their botched engagement – but that she's not very happy with Bernie's lyrics.

What Elton/Long John Said

Elton, commenting on what would have happened, had he actually married Linda: "That would have been goodbye to the music scene for me. I would have been down working at Barclay's Bank or something."

Long John Baldry: "Apparently, I gave Elton some very good advice when he was in a pickle, and he wrote a song about it. But I still can't figure out what the song is about."

Notable covers

The song appears in the trailer for the 2002 film *Moonlight Mile*, and is featured in the film *Hamlet 2*.

Walter Jackson included it on his 1976 album *Feeling Good*.

Mumford & Sons covered the song in the 2018 tribute album *Revamp: Reimagining the Songs of Elton John & Bernie Taupin*.

Factoids

Linda Woodrow got her revenge for this song. When Elton married Renate Blauel, *People* magazine ran a cover story – ELTON JILTED ME – wherein Linda told her side of the story, detailing how bad Elton was in bed, and how he used to wear jewelry and perfume.

"Someone Saved My Life Tonight" was the last single by Elton's classic band in the Seventies. He fired Nigel and Dee after it came out.

Music mogul Tommy Mottola, former husband of Mariah Carey, left her a note that sealed their breakup: "Butterflies are free to fly. Fly away."

The running time is 6:45.

Elton on Top

Song	Position, US	Position, UK
"Crocodile Rock"	#1	#5
"Bennie and the Jets"	#1	
"Lucy in the Sky with Diamonds"	#1	#10
"Philadelphia Freedom"	#1	
"Island Girl"	#1	
"Don't Go Breaking My Heart" (w/ Kiki Dee)	#1	#1
"Sacrifice"		#1
"Don't Let the Sun Go Down on Me" (w/ George Michael)	#1	#1
"Candle in the Wind 1997"	#1	#1
"Are You Ready for Love"		#1
"Rocket Man"	#6	#2
"Daniel"	#2	#4
"Goodbye Yellow Brick Road"	#2	#6
"Don't Let the Sun Go Down on Me"	#2	
"I Don't Wanna Go On with You Like That"	#2	
"True Love" (w/ Kiki Dee)		#2
"Little Jeannie"	#3	
"Nikita"	#7	#3
"The Bitch is Back"	#4	
"Someone Saved My Life Tonight"	#4	
"Song for Guy"		#4
"I Guess That's Why They Call It the Blues"	#4	
"I'm Still Standing"		#4
"Can You Feel the Love Tonight"	#4	
"Your Song" (w/ Alessandro Safina, 2002)		#4
"Electricity"		#4
"Passengers"		#5
"Candle in the Wind" (live)	#6	#5
"Sad Songs (Say So Much)"	#5	#7
"Sorry Seems to Be the Hardest Word"	#6	
"Your Song"	#8	#7
"Saturday Night's Alright for Fighting"		#7
"Pinball Wizard"		#7
"Don't Go Breaking My Heart" (w/ RuPaul, 1994)		#7
"Blue Eyes"		#8
"Honky Cat"	#8	

"Live Like Horses" (w/ Luciano Pavarotti)		#9
"I Want Love"		#9
"Mama Can't Buy You Love"	#9	
"The One"	#9	#10
"Step into Christmas"		#10
"Written in the Stars" (w/ LeAnn Rimes)		#10

Elton's chart life is filled with interesting stuff. Notice that his early years in the US pretty much set the bar: eight #1s there, six of them in a four-year period. He had a much harder time in his homeland, where he didn't have a #1 until "Don't Go Breaking My Heart" – and that was shared with Kiki Dee.

Worse, he had to wait 14 years until he had another one with "Sacrifice".

He hit #1 in both countries with two songs: his "Don't Let the Sun Go Down on Me" duet with George Michael, and his "Candle in the Wind" redux tribute to the departed Princess Diana.

Elton hit #1 twice in the UK with songs that didn't chart at all in the US: "Sacrifice" and "Are You Read for Love", in 2003.

Interestingly, of his Top 10 hits, he had more #1s than anything else: 11. The rest were as follows:

#2 (6)
#3 (2)
#4 (9)
#5 (4)
#6 (4)
#7 (6)
#8 (3)
#9 (4)
#10 (4)

Rock of the Westies

Produced by	Gus Dudgeon
Engineered by	Jeff Geurcio
Performed by	Elton John (vocals, piano) Davey Johnstone (acoustic/electric guitars, slide guitar, banjo, voice bag, backing vocals) Caleb Quaye (acoustic/electric guitars, backing vocals) Kenny Passarelli (bass, vocals) Roger Pope (drums) Ray Cooper (tambourine, cowbell, vibraphone, shaker, kettle drums, congas, bell tree, jawbone, marimba, wind chimes, maracas, castanets) James Newton Howard (ARP synthesizer, harpsichord, mellotron, electric piano, Hohner clavinet) Kiki Dee, Clive Franks, Patti Labelle, Ann Orson (backing vocals)
Released	10/24/1975
Chart Position	#1 (US Billboard 200) / #5 (UK Albums)
Sales	Platinum (US)
Singles	"Island Girl" "Grow Some Funk of Your Own"

Captain Fantastic had debuted at #1, the first album in history to do so.

Rock of the Westies repeated that feat. But it also would be the last in Elton's string of #1 albums that had begun with *Honky Château.*

That said, *Captain Fantastic* was deserving of such success. *Westies* was not. It was rock-oriented, which was fine, but presented uninspired themes, sub-par lyrics, and misguided music. In retrospect, the band's new fascination with cocaine might have adversely affected the quality of its output.

Captain Fantastic -> Westies repeated the pattern of *Yellow Brick Road -> Caribou* – Classic Album followed by Nothing Special.

Westies wasn't a bad album by any means – but it signaled the beginning of the end of Elton's classic era.

Tracks

Side One
> **Medley (Yell Help/Wednesday Night/Ugly**
> > (EJ/Johnstone/Taupin) - 6:13
> **Dan Dare** (EJ/Taupin) - 3:30
> **Island Girl** (EJ/Taupin) - 3:42
> **Grow Some Funk of Your Own** (EJ/Johnstone/Taupin) - 4:43
> **I Feel Like a Bullet (in the Gun of Robert Ford)**
> > (EJ/Taupin) - 5:28

Side Two
> **Street Kids** (EJ/Taupin) - 6:23
> **Hard Luck Story** (Ann Orson/Carte Blanche) - 5:10
> **Feed Me** (EJ/Taupin) - 4:00
> **Billy Bones and the White Bird** (EJ/Taupin) - 4:24

The Writing

Bernie went cynical on *Westies*. "Medley" is an inexplicable retreat into his adolescence, shedding all of his carefully-cultivated maturity, and "Grow Some Funk of Your Own" isn't much better; perhaps this is some kind of self-recrimination, as Bernie was coping with the loss of his wife Maxine, for which he owned up manfully and all-too-vulnerably in "I Feel Like a Bullet (in the Gun of Robert Ford)".

It is safe to place "Island Girl" among Bernie's interesting character portraits, even if he leaned into cliché; "Dan Dare" is more interesting, serving up a childhood hero on a par with Bernie's best cowboy fantasies, and "Hard Luck Story" - which was originally a single for Kiki, though not successful – was at least an earnest attempt by Bernie to dig into the core of marriage.

"Feed Me", a song about the madness of a junkie, is Bernie meeting his own standard, offering up the image that Elton's audience had come to expect. It may be his only truly worthy track on the album, apart from "Bullet".

The Music

Gus Dudgeon recalled arriving at Caribou Ranch for what would be the band's third Caribou recording. It was late at night and he was jet-lagged, but Elton was wide awake in his cabin – which had a piano. Davey, bless his heart, was bunking with Elton, and couldn't sleep with Elton banging away – so he got out of bed and plugged in. Gus listened as they co-wrote the music to "Grow Some Funk of Your Own" and the album's opening "Medley".

The former, in Davey's hands, became straight-up rock – fun, if not particularly interesting.

Elton wisely didn't play on "Feed Me", instead deferring to Ray on vibraphone and James on synth.

The Recording

Recorded in the summer of 1975, Westies was the first album since *Honky Château* that did not feature his core band – Davey, Dee and Nigel. Davey remained, as did percussionist Ray Cooper, but Roger Pope now sat in the drum chair, and David Passarelli held the bass.

"It was a bit tricky," said Gus, "because we were dealing with a different bunch of people."

Said James Newton Howard of serving as Elton's keyboard support: "I think we stimulate each other. When I first joined the band I think it was good for his playing because he's an incredibly competitive person, and I was a sort of a kick in the ass for him. But he certainly was a kick in the ass for me."

The end result is a wall of almost indiscriminate sound, skillfully rendered but unremarkable. It lacks the emotion and nuance of *Westies'* predecessor, and isn't up to the standard of the previous eight albums.

Critical Response

Rock historian Elizabeth Rosenthal, in her musical analysis of the album, concluded that Elton – having dismissed half of a band that had placed him at the top – failed to make use of his new band's potential. He did better on the next album, but by then he had lost the momentum that had sustained him through half of the Seventies.

Stephen Holden, *Rolling Stone*: "...beside the fact that Elton John is a great live entertainer, his records, while commercially essential to his career strategy, have come to seem more and more artistically inconsequential. *Rock of the Westies* is mostly high-energy rock & roll produced by Gus Dudgeon with characteristic gloss. Though the personnel in John's band have changed somewhat, Dudgeon and John have altered only superficially the basic Elton John sound, which is seamlessly mechanistic. *Rock* merely steps up the pace and accentuates the gaudy textures of electric keyboards and synthesizers at the expense of orchestration... Though *Rock of the Westies* gives no clue to the future direction of Elton John, I'm hoping that one of these days he, Bernie Taupin and Gus Dudgeon will make the great album I'm convinced they're capable of."

Rock journalist David Buckley: "*Rock of the Westies* was the sound of a British artist with an Anglo-American band, recording in the United States with an overwhelmingly American sound. To all intents and purposes, it could have been made by an American act."

What Elton Said

Elton: "That period of time is a little foggy because we were all at the high point of abusing ourselves to the max... it was Jack Daniels and lines on the console, and for some reason, we got it done. I don't remember anything about the sessions and I don't think anybody in the band will remember them either, but for some reason, it paid off. Luckily, we're all still alive to tell the tale."

Factoids

It was during the recording of *Westies* that Bernie's wife Maxine, of "Tiny Dancer" fame, left him and moved in with new Elton bassist Kenny Passarelli – inspiring the songs "I Feel Like a Bullet (in the Gun of Robert Ford)" and "Sorry Seems to Be the Hardest Word".

Island Girl

Written by	Elton John, Bernie Taupin
Chart position	#1 (US Billboard Hot 100) / #14 (UK Singles Chart)
Released	9/29/1975
B-side	"Sugar on the Floor"
From the album	*Rock of the Westies*

Elton's fifth #1 single in the US didn't have anything close to the charm or staying power of its predecessors. In fact, it showcased – along with "Grow Some Funk of Your Own", the single that followed – all that was wrong with the album *Rock of the Westies*.

The Writing

Bernie was still writing character songs, which both singles are, but this tune about a New York City prostitute and a man who wants to return her to her native Jamaica doesn't offer any depth or insight – or even concern for its subject.

The one interesting thing about Bernie's lyrics is the style – Bernie wrote the lyrics in Caribbean English.

The Music

Elton gave the music a distinctly tropical feel, giving the other instruments plenty to do – but kept his own piano part at the core of the arrangement. What's interesting is that the musical foundation he wrote is unobtrusive, in spite of its centrality.

The Recording

The recording is all over the place, but has the redeeming quality of being great fun. The song is supposed to evoke Jamaica, but none of the band really focuses. Rock historian Elizabeth Rosenthal points out that

Davey's guitar sounds Hawaiian, and keyboardist James Newton Howard's synthesizer solo has "a generic Caribbean flavoring."

The Response

The song stayed at #1 for three weeks. It eventually went Platinum. Rock biographer Philip Norman called the song, in the context of *Westies*, "a single bright red maraschino cherry among listless tinned grapefruit."

Factoids

"Island Girl" bumped Neil Sedaka's "Bad Blood" from the #1 spot. Sedaka was one of Rocket Records' first artists, and Elton had sung the duet vocal with Sedaka on the song.

The running time is 3:42.

Blue Moves

Produced by	Gus Dudgeon
Engineered by	Arun Chakraverty
Performed by	Elton John (vocals, piano) Davey Johnstone (acoustic/electric guitars, mandolin, slide guitar, dulcimer, sitar) Caleb Quaye (acoustic/electric guitars, 12-string guitar) Kenny Passarelli (bass) Roger Pope (drums) Ray Cooper (tambourine, glockenspiel, vibraphone, bells, marimba, rototom, gong, shaker, triangle, congas, finger cymbals) James Newton Howard (synthesizer, piano, mellotron, electric piano, clavinet) Carl Fortina (accordion) Michael Brecker (saxophone) Randy Brecker (trumpet) David Sanborn (saxophone) Barry Rogers (trombone) Michael Hurwitz (cello) Toni Tennille, David Crosby, Graham Nash, Gene Morford, Ron Hicklin, Cindy Bullens, Clark Burroughs, Joe Chemay, Bruce Johnston, Jon Joyce, Curt Becker (backing vocals) The London Symphony Orchestra The Martyn Ford Orchestra The Gene Page Strings Cornerstone Institutional Baptist Church/Southern California Community Choir (backing vocals) Richard Studt (strings/brass leader) Harry Bluestone (strings leader) Paul Buckmaster (string/brass arrangements) Daryl Dragon (backing vocal arrangements) Rev. James Cleveland (choir director)
Released	10/24/1975
Chart Position	#3 (US Billboard 200) / #3 (UK Albums)
Sales	Platinum (US)

Singles	"Sorry Seems to Be the Hardest Word"
	"Bite Your Lip (Get Up and Dance!)"
	"Crazy Water"

Blue Moves was, to say the least, a transitional album.

Rising only to #3 on the US and UK charts, it ended Elton's lengthy streak of #1 albums, which ran all the way back to *Honky Château.* It ended the even-longer tenure of Gus Dudgeon, who had been in the producer's chair since the *Elton John* album. The Elton/Bernie songwriting partnership ended, at least for a time. And *Blue Moves* ended, ironically, Elton's new-and-improved band, which had only been together since the previous album.

It was Elton's second double album. And while *Goodbye Yellow Brick Road* had been of such high quality that the extra disc was deemed well worth it, one of the great double albums of all time, *Blue Moves* didn't receive nearly that level of patience; despite a number of strong tracks, it was considered to be filler-heavy.

For all that, Elton calls the *Blue Moves* album his favorite.

Tracks

Side One
>**Your Starter For...** (Quaye) - 1:23
>**Tonight** (EJ/Taupin) - 7:52
>**One Horse Town** (EJ/Newton Howard/Taupin) - 5:56
>**Chameleon** (EJ/Taupin) - 5:27

Side Two
>**Boogie Pilgrim** (EJ/Johnstone/Quaye/Taupin) - 6:05
>**Cage the Songbird** (EJ/Johnstone/Taupin) - 3:25
>**Crazy Water** (EJ/Taupin) - 5:42
>**Shoulder Holster** (EJ/Taupin) - 5:10

Side Three
>**Sorry Seems to Be the Hardest Word** (EJ/Taupin) - 3:48
>**Out of the Blue** (EJ/Taupin) - 6:14
>**Between Seventeen and Twenty**
>   (EJ/Johnstone/Quaye/Taupin) - 5:17
>**The Wide Eyed and Laughing**
>   (EJ/Johnstone/Newton Howard/Quaye/Taupin) - 3:27
>**Someone's Final Song** (EJ/Taupin) - 4:10

Side Four
>**Where's the Shoorah?** (EJ/Taupin) - 4:09
>**If There's a God in Heaven (What's He Waiting For?)**
>   (EJ/Johnstone/Taupin) - 4:25
>**Idol** (EJ/Taupin) - 4:08
>**Theme from a Non-Existent TV Show** (EJ/Taupin) - 1:19
>**Bite Your Lip (Get Up and Dance!)** (EJ/Taupin) - 6:43

The Writing

Bernie was at an all-time low while writing the songs that would populate Blue Moves. He had lost his wife to Elton's new bassist Kenny Passarelli, and was beyond bitter about it; his words in "Between Seventeen and Twenty", a song that laments the too-early marriage, scathingly addressed Maxine directly, while simultaneously taking responsibility for the breakup.

 "I never rejected one of his lyrics before but some of the stuff he did for Blue Moves!" Elton remembered. "I said, 'Taupin, for Christ's sake, I can't sing that.' They were just quite painful, three or four of them."

Elton himself contributed to the most painful song of all - "Sorry Seems to Be the Hardest Word", the album's sole successful single[25].

The Music

Elton's music for Bernie's gloomy tunes left wide-open spaces for Paul Buckmaster and the other arrangers. Having decided the album would

---

[25] See " Sorry Seems to Be the Hardest Word", page 158.

be a double in advance of writing it, he built in plenty of space in the songs as he composed.

Davey, who had contributed to the music on a couple of Westies tracks, was credited on tracks on three of *Blue Moves'* four sides – and guitarist Caleb Quaye contributed to four cuts, including the instrumental "Your Starter For...", which opened the album. With keyboardist James Newton Howard also co-writing two tracks, *Blue Moves* was by far the Elton album with the most writers.

Elton himself did two instrumentals, "Out of the Blue" - which felt jazzy – and the goofy "Theme from a Non-Existent TV Series".

The Recording

In contrast to the rock-out of *Westies*, *Blue Moves* was a return to the highly orchestral days of Madman. The London Symphony Orchestra and the Gene Page Strings were called in, as were the Cornerstone Institutional Baptist Church Choir and the Southern California Community Choir. Additional horn players were brought in. Toni Tennille and Beach Boy Bruce Johnstone, both of whom had sung on "Don't Let the Sun Go Down on Me", returned. And the outer two-thirds of Crosby, Stills, and Nash – David and Graham – sang as well.

Though reminiscent of the earliest albums, when dozens of session players had also been common, Blue Moves did break new ground: Elton's balladry on "Sorry" features a gorgeous and melancholy instrumental break, with Ray Cooper blending vibraphone with Carl Fortina's Parisian accordion; "The Wide-Eyed and Laughing" which had an unprecedented five co-writers, had an Asian feel; Davey's influence was indulged on "Songbird", a folkish track that featured dulcimer and the vocals of Crosby and Nash. "Idol" and "Chameleon" had distinctly jazzy flavors.

"Boogie Pilgrim" synthesizes gospel and R&B, while "Crazy Water" and "One Horse Town" tease at modern jazz.

Perhaps the closest Elton gets to his old self, beyond the album's rampant overproduction, is "Tonight", the album's first real track, which presents a melodic power and simplicity reminiscent of "Candle in the Wind". At almost eight minutes, it is the album's longest track, and features a lengthy instrumental break. (It was a natural for inclusion, 11 years later, on the *Live in Australia* album.)

Critical Response

Gus Dudgeon objected to releasing two discs' worth of material, saying there weren't enough quality tunes to justify a double album. Most of the world agreed.

Ariel Swartley, *Rolling Stone*: "While Elton John used to poke fun at rock's poses and pretensions, his playing showed that he took the music seriously enough to quote it well. But times have changed. *Blue Moves* is no different than most double albums in that it contains nowhere near enough good songs to justify the extended length, but songs are no longer the focus. Instead, *Blue Moves* is preoccupied with sound, with instrumental interludes and tidy segues, to the exclusion of sense. It attempts to satisfy the ears while leaving the emotions completely unaroused. In fact, *Blue Moves* is the musical equivalent of a dumb but gorgeous one-night stand. Unfortunately, it is also intended as a sort of farewell album and is clearly meant to have a more lasting effect. Instead it sounds like it's time for John to take a rest."

Robert Christgau: "Impossibly weepy."

What Elton/Bernie Said

Elton: "We were all weary, feeling pressure and needed a break. Out of those situations comes rawness, and some of the lyrics are real desperate. I just love the album."

Factoids

Blue Moves was the first Elton album released on his own Rocket Records label, following the expiration of his recording contract with DJM.

The cover art is a reprint of Patrick Procktor's painting *The Guardian Readers*, which hung in Elton's Woodside home. The press noted, with raised eyebrow, that all the human figures in the painting are male.

Don't Go Breaking My Heart

Written by	Ann Orson, Carte Blanche
Chart position	#1 (US Billboard Hot 100) / #1 (UK Singles Chart)
Released	6/21/1976
B-side	"Snow Queen"

Elton's 1976 duet with Kiki Dee was the first of many he'd do in the coming years – and was an extreme departure, in both style and presentation, from all that had come before.

Credited to "Ann Orson" and "Carte Blanche", the song was of course written by Elton and Bernie – but they used pseudonyms because Elton had actually written the first draft of the lyrics.

And though the song is conceived as a duet, Kiki Dee was not their first choice for recording it. They had intended to do the song with Dusty Springfield, but she turned out to be too sick at that time to do it.

It's just as well: Elton's performance with Kiki Dee is, at this point, iconic – and she and Elton had, at that point, been friends for years. She was his protégé, and had been his opening act during his 1974 tour.

The Writing

"I was messing around in the studio...on the electric piano and came up with the title line," Elton said. "I made a hasty call to Barbados [where Bernie was staying] and said, 'Write a duet,' and Taupin nearly died 'cause he'd never done one."

"We were in Barbados for Christmas, and [Elton] came to me and said, 'I really want to write something up-tempo, like a disco-soul thing,'" Bernie said. "So I went upstairs and started banging away on the typewriter. In five minutes, I'd done something, came downstairs, and just gave it to him. In the next five minutes, he'd finished it, and it was great. It was just one of those things that sparked off immediately. As soon as he played it, I said, 'Well, that's gonna be the next single. That's a hit!"

Bernie didn't exactly nail the lyrics the first time, however: the familiar man-woman back-and-forth, each singer answering the other, wasn't present when they started recording Elton's part in Toronto.

"I was with Elton in Canada and he actually sang about three quarters of the song, and gave Kiki about four lines," said producer Gus Dudgeon. "I said, 'Hang on a minute, is this supposed to be a duet or a guest appearance?' Elton replied, 'A duet.' 'Then you've got to give her at least 50 percent of the song!'"

The Music

Elton's music for the tune was to evoke Motown, in particular the style of man/woman duets that many of its artists had made popular.

"Both Elton and I were big fans of those duets on Motown by the likes of Marvin Gaye and Tammi Terrell," said Kiki in *1000 UK #1 Hits*, "and as there hadn't been any around for a bit, we thought we'd do one ourselves."

Gus Dudgeon remembered Elton conceiving the song at a piano in the studio, with no Bernie lyric to work from: "All he was singing was 'Don't go breaking my heart,' 'Don't go breaking my heart,' 'Don't go breaking my heart,' 'Don't go breaking my heart,' 'Don't go breaking my heart...' That's what he sang all the way through!" First draft, indeed.

The Recording

Once Elton's vocals were recorded in Toronto, the tapes were forwarded to Kiki in London, where her vocals were added.

"Elton had recorded the song abroad," she remembered, "and also did my vocals in a high-pitched voice which was quite funny, so I knew which lines to sing." The backing vocals, by Kiki, Curt Boettcher and

Cindy Bullens, were recorded during the *Blue Moves* sessions in Toronto.

The song was the first single Elton recorded after the firing of Nigel Olsson and Dee Murray. Davey Jonestone was on guitar, Ray Cooper on percussion, alongside new band members James Newton Howard on keys (he also did the orchestral arrangement), Kenny Passarelli on bass, and Roger Pope on drums.

The Response

"Don't Go Breaking My Heart" was Elton's long-awaited first #1 in his homeland. He would not have another until "Sacrifice" in 1990.

It also went to #1 in the US – his last there until "Candle in the Wind 1997".

It was the second-best selling song of 1976 in both countries.

Elton and Kiki went on to perform the song at Live Aid in 1985.

What Elton/Kiki Said

"I remember hearing it on the radio for the first time and thinking, 'Wow.'" said Kiki. "'Cause some records, especially in those days, they have to sound great on the radio…and this was one of those records that did. I remember thinking, 'Oh, this could do okay…this could go.'"

"When I heard it was number one (in Britain) I rang everybody I knew to tell them," Elton said. "They were pretty annoyed, but, hell, it got me excited again. It really did."

"People have got a lot of fondness for that song," said Kiki. "I did a guest spot at a big music festival…and when the other acts were playing I went out into the audience. A lot of people told me how much the song meant to them. One was an Indian guy who'd come over in 1972, and 'Don't Go Breaking My Heart' was his favorite song ever. It was very, very sweet."

Factoids

Elton has subsequently performed the song with a number of other partners, including Miss Piggy, Minnie Mouse, and RuPaul. He performed it again with Kiki Dee at Madison Square Garden in 2000, in a performance captured in the concern film *Elton John One Night Only – The Greatest Hits*.

Elton and Kiki considered recording a cover of the Four Tops tune "Loving You is Sweeter Than Ever". They did record another duet, finally, in 1993 – a cover of "True Love", which went to #2 in the UK.

Kiki Dee was a Rocket Records artist before she was approached to do the song, having charted with Rocket albums *Amoureuse* and *I've Got the Music in Me*. Elton produced both albums.

Kiki Dee had a relationship with Davey Johnstone from 1977 to 1979. Kiki was at that time a tax exile, and they shared an apartment in Los Angeles. Their break-up was amicable, more to do with her wanting to return home to England than anything else.

Originally released on *Greatest Hits Vol. II* (but later removed for copyright reasons), "Don't Go Breaking My Heart" can be found on *Greatest Hits 1976-1986*, *Elton John's Greatest Hits 1970-2002*, and *Diamonds*.

The orchestration, by band keyboardist James Newton Howard, used 12 violins, four violas and four cellos.

Kiki Dee's real name is Pauline Mathews.

Every year, Elton sends Kiki an orchid in a pot for her birthday – and every year she makes a donation to his AIDS foundation in return.

The running time is 4:28.

Sorry Seems to Be the Hardest Word

Written by	Elton John, Bernie Taupin
Chart position	#6 (US Billboard Hot 100) / #11 (UK Singles Chart)
Released	11/1/1976
B-side	"Shoulder Holster"
From the album	*Blue Moves*

"Sorry Seems to Be the Hardest Word", Elton's hymn of heartbreak and mourning, is a masterpiece.

Recorded during the *Blue Moves* sessions, it was a complete departure from the themes and sound that had defined his ascent in the pop/rock pantheon. It isn't just a sad, sad song; it's a lamentation, a cry of anguish, one so artfully and movingly put forth that it elevates Elton and partner Bernie Taupin into the company of their Liverpool countrymen, Lennon and McCartney.

The Writing

Bernie Taupin's lyric, which captures the deep ache of a failing relationship, bookends his first marriage - the ending of his time with his wife Maxine Feibelman, the real-life Tiny Dancer. It is not, however, his eulogy of the marriage; he wrote that into the song "I Feel Like a Bullet (in the Gun of Robert Ford)", from the previous album, *Rock of the Westies*. In that song, he regretfully accepted responsibility for his mistakes; this song is simply a snapshot of the sorrow he was feeling at the time.

Critical Analysis

It is difficult if not impossible to discuss the music and lyric separately, so seamlessly are they integrated. They are both deeply melancholy, evoking isolation and hopelessness. Elton's melody line in the verse is mid-range, a speaking pitch rather than his usual ebullient tenor, as he asks questions of his love, who isn't there to listen:

"What have I gotta do to make you love me,
What have I gotta do to make you care?
What do I do when lightning strikes me,
And I wake to find that you're not there?"

Strings swell beneath Elton's dirging piano pulse, as he continues:

"What I have I gotta do to make you want me,
What have I gotta do to be heard?
What do I say when it's all over,
And Sorry seems to be the hardest word?"

The music is perfect here. The song is in the unlikely key of Gm, to accommodate Elton's sober baritone, and the chords rise and fall slowly: Gm-Cm, F-Bb, and back again, like ocean waves at night.

The song connects immediately, because this lyric defines, in the darkest terms, heartbreak - unimaginable loss. Most of us have been there.

The chorus boosts the stakes, as Elton sings,

"It's sad, so sad (so sad),
It's a sad, sad situation..."

That's *five 'sads' in five seconds* - over-the-top Victorian melodrama, and Elton's voice climbs into his trademark falsetto for the first time, accentuating the exaggeration of the moment, which he surprisingly affirms in the next line:

"...and it's gettin' more and more absurd..."

The music here is perfect. The chorus begins on Gm, descending through a progression to D/F#, F, and C/E, with a down-stepping high note: the singer is slowly falling into an abyss, and now Elton's falsetto - emerging on the words "sad, sad situation" - evokes not melodrama but anguish. This progression repeats - he is falling, over and over - but this time he asks,

"Why can't we talk it over?"

- implying that he and his love haven't yet done so, and now
the crescendoing melody underscores his frustration; the relationship
is foundering on communication, not a lapse of love, and a final,
damning failure:

"Oh, it seems to me, that Sorry seems to be the hardest word..."

Pride is holding back the reconciliation of the relationship the singer is
longing to restore.

The coda lands the song right in the crack of the broken heart, as Elton
repeats his *"What have I gotta do?"* one last time, now in his falsetto
melody - reaching desperately.

Here's where it gets *really* interesting. Not all of the lyrics were
Taupin's; Elton added some of his own. On top of that, he wrote most
of the music without the words in front of him. Both events are
exceptional, in the context of their partnership.

Elton and Bernie are no strangers to tone poems - "Your Song", which
got the world's attention, is a perfect exemplar - and this one is more
perfect still. It solemnly records the sound of a breaking heart.

The Recording

Unlike Elton's previous singles, this one wasn't done with his band. It
was recorded by Elton on his piano, an orchestra playing an
arrangement by James Newton Howard, with longtime EJ
percussionist Ray Cooper playing a vibraphone solo between the
choruses, with Carl Fortina on accordion.

Greatest Hits

The song is, very ironically, back-to-back with "Don't Go Breaking My
Heart" in Elton's singles sequence, and the two songs were the first
two singles released on his own Rocket Records label. Both were
included on *Greatest Hits Volume II*. As Rocket singles, however, they

did not provide royalties to Dick James Music, which had owned Elton's and Bernie's copyrights up to that time. And so they were replaced on the 1992 redux version of the album, very ironically, by "Tiny Dancer" and "I Feel Like a Bullet (in the Gun of Robert Ford)" - the actual story of the marriage that broke Bernie's heart. (Both songs appear on Elton's subsequent compilations.)

Notable Covers

The song has been covered by Joe Cocker, Frank Sinatra, Chet Atkins/ Susie Bogguss, Blue, Ray Charles, Mary J. Blige, Kenny G/Richard Marx, Jimmy Scott, Diana Krall and Pedro Aznar.

End of an Era

For many fans, this song ended an era. As the last song recorded of those appearing on *Greatest Hits II*, it wraps up the Early Elton or Classic Elton years, as EJ's sound and themes drifted away from the Yellow Brick Road vibe into the less exuberant, more contemplative early Eighties idiom of "Little Jeannie", "Blue Eyes" and "Empty Garden". To such fans, that 1970-1977 period, from "Your Song" to this song, represents True Elton - an era that has never been repeated.

Appendix: Honors

The Grammy Hall of Fame inducts songs and albums, not people. Winners of Elton's and Bernie's include:

Elton John (1970)
"Your Song" (1970)
Goodbye Yellow Brick Road (1973)

The *Lion King* songs Elton wrote with Tim Rice received three Academy Award Nominations, all for Best Original Song.

"Can You Feel the Love Tonight" won. "Circle of Life" and "Hakuna Matata" were the other songs nominated.

"Can You Feel the Love Tonight" also won the 1994 Golden Globe Award for Best Original Song.

Elton and Tim Rice also won the 2000 Tony Award for Best Original Score for *Aida*. Elton received Tony nominations for *The Lion King*, *Billy Elliot the Musical*, and *Next Fall*.

Elton was awarded the Society of Singers Lifetime Achievement Award in 2005.

He received the Disney Legends Award in 2006.

"Daniel" won Ivor Novello Best Song Musically and Lyrically in 1974.

"Don't Go Breaking My Heart" won Ivor Novello Best Pop Song in 1977, and was nominated for International Hit of the Year and Most Performed Work.

"Song for Guy" won Ivor Novello Best Instrumental in 1979.

Elton won Ivor Novello Outstanding Contribution to British Music in 1979.

"Nikita" was nominated for Ivor Novello International Hit of the Year in 1986.

"Nikota" won Best Song Musically and Lyrically in 1986.

"Sacrifice" won Ivor Novello Best Song Musically and Lyrically in 1991.

"Sacrifice" won Ivor Novello Best Selling A-side in 1991.

"Circle of Life" won Ivor Novello Best Song Included in Film, 1995.

"Candle in the Wind" won Ivor Novello Best-Selling UK Single in 1998.

Elton won the 2000 Ivor Novello award for International Achievement in Musical Theater.

"I Don't Feel Like Dancin'" won Ivor Novello Most Performed Work in 2007, but lost International Hit of the Year, for which it was nominated.

Appendix: At the Grammys

WIN: *"That's What Friends Are For"*
1987, Best Performance by a Duo or Group with Vocal

WIN: "Basque"
1992, Best Instrumental Composition

WIN: "Can You Feel the Love Tonight"
1995, Best Song Written for a Motion Picture

WIN: "Candle in the Wind 1997"
1998, Best Male Pop Vocal Performance

WIN: Grammy Legend Award
1999

WIN: Best Musical Show Award
2001, *Elton John & Tim Rice's Aida*

NOMINATED: 1971, Best New Artist

NOMINATED: *Elton John*
1971, Album of the Year

NOMINATED: *Elton John*
1971, Best Contemporary Male Vocalist

NOMINATED: *Friends*
1972, Best Original Score Written for a Motion Picture

NOMINATED: "Daniel"
1974, Best Male Pop Vocal Performance

NOMINATED: "Don't Let the Sun Go Down on Me"
1975, Record of the Year

NOMINATED: *Caribou*
1975, Album of the Year

NOMINATED: *Captain Fantastic and the Brown Dirt Cowboy*
1976, Best Male Pop Vocal Performance

NOMINATED: "Don't Go Breaking My Heart"
1977, Best Male Pop Vocal Performance
NOMINATED: "Mama Can't Buy You Love"
1980, Best R&B Vocal Performance

NOMINATED: "Blue Eyes"
1983, Best Male Pop Vocal Performance

NOMINATED: "Restless"
1985, Best Male Pop Vocal Performance

NOMINATED: "That's What Friends Are For"
1987, Record of the Year

NOMINATED: "Candle in the Wind (live)"
1988, Best Male Pop Performance

NOMINATED: "Don't Let the Sun Go Down on Me" with George
Michael
1993, Best Pop Performance by a Duo or Group

NOMINATED: "The One"
1993, Best Male Pop Vocal Performance

NOMINATED: "Can You Feel the Love Tonight"
1995, Song of the Year

NOMINATED: "Circle of Life"
1995, Best Song Written Specificallly for a Motion Picture
1995, Song of the Year

NOMINATED: "Believe"
1996, Best Male Pop Vocal Performance

NOMINATED: *Songs from the West Coast*
2002, Best Pop Vocal Album

NOMINATED: "I Want Love"

2002, Best Male Pop Vocal Performance

NOMINATED: "Original Sin"
2003, Best Male Pop Vocal Performance

NOMINATED: "Sorry Seems to Be the Hardest Word" (w/ Ray Charles)
2005, Best Pop Collaboration with Vocals

NOMINATED: "If It Wasn't for Bad"
2011, Best Pop Collaboration with Vocals

Sources / Bibliography

Magazine/newspaper Sources

"Bernie Taupin on 48 Years Writing With Elton John and Their New LP", *Rolling Stone*, November 17, 2015

"Elton John and Bernie Taupin Look Back At 'Goodbye Yellow Brick Road'", *Rolling Stone*, March 14, 2014

"Guitarist Davey Johnstone Looks Back on His Five-Decade Odyssey With Elton John", *Rolling Stone*, September 7, 2018

"Nigel Olsson Reflects on 50 Years of Playing Drums for Elton John," *Rolling Stone*, August 22, 2018

Book Sources

Elton: The Biography, David Buckley. Chicago Review Press, 2007.

Elton John: In His Own Words, Susan Black. Omnibus Press, 1993.

His Song: The Musical Journal of Elton John, Elizabeth J. Rosenthal. Billboard Books, 2001.

Love is the Cure: On Life, Loss, and the End of AIDS, Elton John. Atlantik Verlag, 2014.

Me, Elton John. Henry Holt and Co., 2019.
Sir Elton: The Definitive Biography, Philip Norman. Carroll & Graf, 1991, 2000.

Video Sources

Elton John: Goodbye Yellow Brick Road, Classic Albums, 2001

169

Elton John: Goodbye Yellow Brick Road, Classic Albums, 2001

About the Author

Scott Robinson is a journalist, social scientist and musician living in the US Midwest. He was a music critic for the *Louisville Courier-Journal* for 20 years, and has been published in *Rolling Stone* and the *Wall Street Journal*. He is the author of *Rock Candy: The Beatles*, *Rock Candy: Elton John*, *The Progressive Beatles* and *YesTales*. He is also the author of more that 25 additional books, covering topics ranging from *Star Trek* to artificial intelligence. He can be found at

www.facebook.com/scottrobinson99

9 798594 193970